Get Out of the Way!

How to Identify and Avoid a Driver Under the Influence

Doug Thorburn

Galt Publishing
Northridge, California

PUBLISHED BY GALT PUBLISHING
P.O. Box 7777, Northridge, CA 91327-7777

"Drug Addiction Recognition Expert"
is trademarked by Doug Thorburn

Address the author c/o Galt Publishing
or at PrevenTragedy@mindspring.com

Cover design and illustration by Lightbourne © 2002
Inside illustrations by Bryan Botton © 2002

CFP® and Certified Financial Planner® are marks owned by the
Certified Financial Planner Board of Standards, Inc.

Publisher's Cataloging-in-Publication

Thorburn, Doug.
    Get out of the way! how to identify and
avoid a driver under the influence / by Doug
Thorburn. -- 1st ed.
    p. cm.

    ISBN: 0-9675788-4-1
    Includes bibliographical references and index.

    1. Substance abuse--Popular works.
2. Alcoholism 3. Drug abuse.   I. Title.
RC564.29.T46 2002   362.29

Table of Contents

Table of Figures

Acknowledgements

This book could not have been written without the aid of countless recovering addicts as well as authors, many of whom helped me understand the nature of the disease of alcoholism. The great authorities include most of those listed in my previous book, *Drunks, Drugs & Debits*, but in particular I wish to acknowledge addiction experts and authors James Graham, Katherine Ketcham and James Milam for shedding light on the misbehaviors of practicing alcoholics in-between drinking episodes. The late Vernon E. Johnson and Harry M. Tiebout, M.D., also provided invaluable insights into the distortions that every alcoholic experiences.

I also wish to thank those who read and provided critiques for early drafts, including my good friends Melvin J. Kreger, Esquire, and David Botton, along with Drug Recognition Officers Thomas Page, Donald Boon and one other who prefers to remain anonymous, but who was instrumental in helping me stay focused on the subject at hand. I also wish to thank my illustrator Bryan Botton and extraordinary assistant Jennifer Huddleston for converting this work into publishable format.

A Special Acknowledgement

My editor, Scott Dorfman, has been given the extraordinary gift of being able to translate my meaning in a way that allows the reader to understand ideas as I intend. After I plodded through change after change in rewriting the manuscript, he was often able to visualize entire paragraphs as they should be. If it weren't for his ability, you might not be reading this book. For this, hopefully my reader will join me in extending sincere and heartfelt thanks.

Ironically, a traffic ticket that I received is what brought us together. He was my instructor at traffic school. After watching and listening to him for only a half-hour, I realized that he would be a great editor. This was due to knowledge of Psychological Type and Temperament that I learned from David Keirsey's work. Scott had previously edited only minor articles, but has done an amazing job editing my prior book (*Drunks, Drugs & Debits: How to Recognize Addicts and Avoid Financial Abuse*) and now, this one.

I hope to have the opportunity to work with Scott in future endeavors. It is an honor, and a privilege.

Foreword

By Sergeant Thomas Page,
Drug Recognition Expert, Sergeant, LAPD, ret.

Sir Issac Newton's first law of motion, inertia, states that a body in motion continues to move in the same direction unless acted upon by an outside force. This basic law of physics applies to the predictable pattern of alcohol and other drug addiction. There's an old saying in the rehabilitation field: an addict will continue using alcohol and other drugs until it becomes easier to quit than to continue. There is also a maxim that addicts won't ask for help until they hit "bottom." For some, this is not reached until they land on Skid Row. Unfortunately, by the time they have sunk this low, there isn't much inducement to change because they have nothing left to lose. Yet for others, this "bottom" is reached much earlier, when all is not yet lost. Many recovering addicts report that crises of varying magnitudes motivated them to "try" sobriety. Such crises include a spouse making a credible threat of divorce, a supervisor initiating discipline for unsatisfactory work performance, a physician warning of adverse health consequences, or an arrest and conviction for driving under the influence.

The path of addiction typically results in the loss of self-respect, employment, savings, family, friends, hygiene and health. For many, law enforcers, particularly traffic specialists, have been the opposing force that stops the body in motion from continuing on this predictable, downward spiraling path. An arrest for DUI has served as a wake-up call that finally forces the individual into treatment and eventual recovery. Many are enrolled in rehabilitation programs because of such an intervention by the criminal justice system.

Over my approximately twenty-five years in law enforcement, there has been a revolutionary change in attitudes over drinking and driving. "Have one for the road," is now an anachronism, just

as "Who's the designated driver?" would have resulted in per-
plexed looks not too many years ago. Thanks in large part to
organizations such as Mothers Against Drunk Driving, driving
under the influence is no longer something to laugh about. Judges
believed to be lenient in the sentencing of intoxicated drivers risk
the wrath of MADD, voters and the media. Law enforcement, too,
has begun to change its priorities. Until only recently, a DUI arrest
in some agencies was looked upon with disdain by the arresting
officer's colleagues and supervisors. Many officers routinely let
drunk drivers go if they were stopped only a few blocks from
home. They were also known to tell such drivers to walk, call a
cab, sleep it off or drive home very carefully.

Fortunately, this sort of lenient DUI enforcement is mostly in
the past. The majority of officials are now committed to making
DUI arrests a priority. Tougher sentencing, mandatory license rev-
ocation and lowered illegal blood alcohol levels, along with
devices such as the ignition interlock, support such officers in their
efforts to get DUIs off the streets. One of the most significant
changes has been the lowering of the statutorily defined level of
DUI. There is a good chance that all 50 states will change their DUI
legal limit to .08 percent by 2005. However, in Sweden, the legal
limit is .02 percent. They are truly saying, "Don't drink and drive."
Here, we really mean, "Don't drink too much and drive." We also
tell people to "Think when you drink." The trouble is, people who
drink alcoholically--those with whom we must be most con-
cerned--have their thinking altered. "Think before you drink" is
what we should be saying. While we are moving in the right direction, there is still a long way to go.

However, improvements will continue. We have already seen
the degree to which advertising helps. A permuted "Don't drink
and drive" is a common slogan in many countries. Some courts
have mandated that automobiles registered to repeat DUI offend-
ers bear identifying tags, meant to both dissuade the person from
driving while impaired and to embarrass him or her into submis-
sion to the law. The phrase Community Oriented Policing, or COP,
is a relatively new concept. COP represents the notion that police
and citizens need to work together to achieve lasting success in
suppressing, as well as preventing, crime. Initially, many law
enforcement officials found the notion that citizens could have a
role in their mission anathema. "Leave policing to the profession-

als" was their mantra. Fortunately, this attitude, once frozen solid in much of the law enforcement community, has since thawed. Most officers now fully accept the concept that the best, most effective policing comes about when they work with community members as partners.

This idea is now being taken another major step forward. I have found Doug Thorburn's book remarkable in many ways. The first is that it was not written by a law enforcement officer, but instead by a concerned, passionate and articulate citizen. I believe that Doug has seen not only the forest, but also the trees of the DUI problem. He has applied common sense to it, rather than relying on jargon, legalese, or bureaucratic gobbledygook. His methods of identification, rooted in the observation that behavior problems are usually a result of substance addiction, add considerably to our understanding of this disorder. These methods substantially improve the odds of detection and subsequent intervention by close persons and the law. The public policy suggestions are also particularly significant. Although some are controversial, as a whole I think he has balanced the ideals of a free society with the need to ensure public safety on the roads.

I commend Doug for his enlightened and practical insights into the mind and behaviors of the impaired driver. This book will be a valuable addition to drivers' training schools, traffic schools, police academies and automobile clubs. Police officers, policy makers and citizens alike will find this book innovative, enlightening and stimulating.

Foreword

by Forest Tennant, M.D., Dr.P.H.

Be prepared for a startling and insightful drive on the road of alcohol and other drug addiction. Doug Thorburn is directing traffic on his trip down "Crusade Boulevard" and we'd all better get on board. It may even save your life. Thorburn makes his case simply but eloquently. He demonstrates that it is not just the visible inebriation or physical impairment of the addict that's important, but also the personality that's affecting our lives much more than we realize, both on and off the highway. The reality is, signs of physical impairment are often invisible, but the behaviors are obvious if one knows what to observe. The biological personality and chemical make-up of the addict produces a litany of both self and other destructive behaviors. For our protection we need to be able to identify addicts, because they are found all too frequently in our family and business lives. Thorburn teaches us how to spot the behaviors indicative of addiction.

You'll pick up an astounding array of lifesaving tips on avoiding the alcoholic behind the wheel. For example, the person behind the tinted glass, always on the mobile phone, or constantly in a hurry may be the very addict who runs you down when you least expect it. An essential element of this book is a clear explanation of how the genetic and biological defect in the alcoholic causes toxins to form in the brain, which in turn creates very poor judgment even when the alcoholic is not drinking. This allows him to believe that he can "do no wrong," which then leads him to drive while under the influence, or worse. The bottom line message of Thorburn's work is that we should stop looking for obvious signs of inebriation and look instead to the behaviors. We need to learn that at some point the alcoholic will turn destructive, often behind the wheel of a car. Unfortunately, it takes more than sweet talk to make an addict change.

Preface

My name is Doug Thorburn. By profession, I'm a tax and financial professional (Enrolled Agent and Certified Financial Planner licensee). You may be asking yourself why a non-addict is writing a book on identifying Drivers Under the Influence (DUIs) when he is not a therapist, doctor, psychiatrist or even a person in law enforcement. It's a long story, but I'll try to keep it short.

Several years ago, I was romantically involved with an alcoholic. I survived the ordeal (barely) and, vowing never to go through anything like that again, decided I'd better learn a little something about addiction. I happened upon some Alcoholics Anonymous meetings and realized that was a good place to start. I ended up attending scores of meetings, interviewing hundreds of recovering addicts and reading almost as many books on the subject.

In the process, I began doing something that appears to have been unique. I found myself tentatively identifying addiction where it wasn't even suspected based on repeated financial misbehaviors. I broadened this idea to include all misbehaviors committed in serial fashion. I eventually realized that I was on to something that seemed quite simple: if addiction causes distorted perceptions resulting in impaired judgments and manifests in observably destructive behaviors, the concept could be reversed. Where these behaviors were observed, I usually found addiction.

Thus my first book, *Drunks, Drugs & Debits: How to Recognize Addicts and Avoid Financial Abuse* was born. In it, I explain why we need to identify alcohol and other drug addicts, how to do so based on behavior patterns and actions to take to *prevent* tragedy in all areas of one's life. However, I came to realize that many people are reluctant to intervene in the lives of those to whom they are close. So, I began to ponder the idea that more headway might be made by encouraging people to help the addict experience consequences when *not* personally known to them and in the area where they are most apparent and lethal: the road. This book is the result.

Introduction

One day in late July 2000, a tow-truck operator was called to pull a pickup out of hood-deep water in a lake fed by Portage Glacier near Anchorage, Alaska. The owner of the pickup, Robert Richardson, told tow operator John Sheedy that he'd driven into the lake in a failed attempt to turn around. Sheedy noticed that Richardson staggered, slurred his speech, had trouble following directions and reeked of alcohol. When the tow operator told Richardson that he appeared too drunk to drive and threatened to take his keys, Richardson responded that he didn't think Sheedy had the legal authority to do so. Sheedy, much to his regret, let the intoxicated man drive off.

A few miles down the road 15-year old Kevin Blake, driving on his learner's permit with his 11-year old cousin Kenneth Kramer and grandparents David and Patsy Glassen, was heading towards Portage Glacier. "What's that guy doing, Gramps?" were the last words Kevin said, as he saw a pickup suddenly veering into their lane no more than 40 feet away. Trying to avoid a collision, Kevin swerved to the right and accelerated. Unfortunately, the pickup was driving too fast and the ensuing crash tore off Kevin's door. The grandparents sustained injuries, but lived. Both boys died at the scene. The driver of the pickup, who survived, was Robert Richardson.[1]

In another tragedy, a driver called 911 to report a van driving erratically on Pacific Coast Highway in Malibu, California. Minutes later, the van crashed into a car carrying two Pepperdine University law students, killing them both. The van's driver, who had been convicted of drunk driving five years earlier, only suffered a sprained ankle. He was found to be under the influence.[2]

Events like these occur an average of 30 times a day in the United States. Most of those responsible demonstrate many behavioral clues that suggest a drinking or other drug problem long before anyone is maimed or killed. Even just before these events occur, there are often many witnesses to driving behaviors that could have predicted impending disaster. If these bystanders were shown how to identify addicts (which include those addicted to the drug alcohol) combined with a system of law that acts as an intervener, many of these tragedies would be prevented. The key is to understand the need to identify addiction far earlier than is typical and to respond appropriately. For this to occur, both non-addict and recovering addict observers need to:

(1) understand that addiction is a biological disorder, causing the afflicted to engage in reckless and destructive conduct,

(2) accept the fact that practicing addicts, regardless of how good they can be when sober, will--not may, but will--misbehave in ways that could be lethal to others,

(3) learn the identifying signs of addiction and

(4) not only stop protecting addicts from the consequences of their misbehaviors, but also proactively assist them in experiencing proper outcomes.

Every year, intoxicated drivers in the United States are responsible for 20,000 deaths, hundreds of thousands of injuries and tens of billions of dollars in property damage. Most of us know, or have ourselves been victims to such impaired drivers. If we identify them, we can get out of their way and keep a safe distance. By doing what we can to take such impaired drivers off the road we help to avoid tragedies. This saves lives, prevents injuries, reduces property damage and decreases the cost of insurance for everyone.

However, removing these "Driver(s) Under the Influence" (DUIs, or DWIs—Driving While Intoxicated) from behind the wheel is not only very difficult, but also very rare. The 911 reporting system is far from perfect, with few calls resulting in stopping (let alone arresting) suspected DUIs. According to visitors at Portage Glacier, where Robert Richardson had walked six miles to report his pickup stuck in the lake, law enforcers had been notified about a possible drunk driver. There seems to have been plenty of time for authorities to act during the walk back and subsequent wait for the tow truck. There was also a several hour period preceding his failed turnabout, when he had probably begun to drink himself into oblivion. He was obviously driving part of that time, yet there were no prior reports to 911. We will find that both Richardson and the driver of the van in Malibu likely exhibited many behaviors indicative of driving under the influence during the hours before they were finally reported.

Furthermore, few in law enforcement have taken the specialized training that not only teaches them how to identify a DUI, but also to prove this to the satisfaction of a court. While surprising to the sober among us, the U.S. Department of Transportation somberly states, "Some officers are not highly skilled at DWI detection. They fail to recognize and arrest many DWI violators."[3] Unfortunately, this contention is supported in a landmark Fort Lauderdale, Florida study. In the study, traffic violators cited by police officers, but not suspected of DUI, were about to get back on the road. Researchers then administered breath tests to these drivers. For every 10 DUIs the original citing officers arrested, the researchers found 37 more that the police missed.[4] This would not shock most addicts, many of whom have been confronted by a law enforcement officer at one time or another while legally under the influence without experiencing repercussions.

Although the legal system has greatly improved in the area of DUI enforcement since the founding of Mothers Against Drunk Driving in 1980, it still doesn't deal with the problem as it should. In many cases, lawyers simply doing their jobs are instrumental in protecting alcoholics from the consequences of their actions. The law itself must be changed to remedy this situation. Due to perceived conflicts with civil liberties, it may be challenging, but not impossible.

Worse yet, there are so many intoxicated drivers, identifying even a small percentage of them would temporarily overwhelm the criminal justice system. As many as 2% of drivers (one out of every fifty) are legally drunk or incapacitated on weekdays, 5% on weekday nights/weekend days and 10% on weekend nights.[5] With numbers of this magnitude, it's hard to believe there isn't more carnage on the roads.

According to the U.S. Department of Transportation the average DUI violator (which we will show is almost always an alcoholic) drinks and drives above the legal limit at least eighty times per year.[6] It is believed that the *average* non-alcoholic almost never does so after his college years. The odds, then, greatly favor a DUI arrest for an alcoholic over a non-alcoholic, since the latter rarely drinks and drives. Therefore, if there is a second DUI arrest, the likelihood of a person having the disease of alcoholism is virtually

100%. As the Johnson Institute (now merged into Hazelden) puts it, "The *non*alcoholic might have *one* brush with the law. He might have *one* reprimand from his employer. He might have family problems over *one* drinking episode. But one such event would be enough to make him say to himself, 'If I'm going to have *that* kind of trouble, I'm going to have to limit my drinking.' And the person will. The alcoholic, to the contrary, will continue to use the chemical even though it causes *continuing problems*...."[7] Because there is a far lower innate tolerance to alcohol in non-alcoholics, there is a higher probability of a near accident occurring during a given period of driving under the influence. Since a close call could be considered a form of "trouble," this would likely serve to limit the drinking and, even more, the occasions for doing so and driving. Therefore, it is the ways, styles, behaviors and methods of the *alcoholic* with which we must become familiar in order to increase our chances of identifying and properly dealing with a problem that puts us all at risk.

Unfortunately, the chances of getting caught are remote. The average DUI is arrested only once in every 500 to 2000 incidents.[8] The statistical probabilities for the average alcoholic being convicted then, are only once every six to twenty-five years. The low DUI arrest rate is not a strong deterrent, even to the rational thinking person which, of course, the addict is not.

The suffering of consequences not only helps to make the roads safer for the rest of us, but in the long run, also helps addicts. Consequences create pain, helping to create crises, which in turn set the stage for intervention. Many addicts report that they got sober at least in part because of the financial, business and personal problems occasioned by an arrest for DUI. Furthermore, a conviction often serves as the single most powerful tool to bring about abstinence. Where the law has required sobriety in exchange for reduced penalties and imprisonment, the rate of recovery has dramatically improved.

This "coerced abstinence" is the legal equivalent of intervention. A more personal version consists of two to eight close people (family, friends, coworkers and/or teachers) and a chemical dependency counselor in a private setting. This needs to be done due to distorted, self-favoring perceptions that cause the addict to become incapable of making the connection between his use of substances and the problems they cause (for everyone). An intervention is one way to forge this link for him.

In an intervention, the addict is offered a choice of sobriety or further consequences. It may seem obvious, but it is essential to note that if there have been no consequences, this choice can't exist. Therefore, problems, mistakes and misbehaviors must be allowed to escalate into crises. If the addict has experienced enough pain and chooses to avoid more of the same, he will decide to make an attempt to not drink or use. It doesn't matter that he kicks and screams all the way to AA, other treatment or white knuckles it by himself. He doesn't immediately come to believe that he has the disease of alcoholism; instead, a buildup of crises leaves him no choice but to try abstinence. After a period of time in which the brain has a chance to heal (usually six to eighteen months), abstinence turns into sobriety. It is only then that normal behaviors begin to resume and a growing acceptance of the need to permanently remain sober occurs. Close persons should understand and accept that this never happens immediately, regardless of what the addict might say or do.

Crises include the following, resulting from impaired judgments caused by alcoholism:
  · loss of job or demotion
  · separation from spouse or significant other
  · separation from/removal of children
  · divorce
  · threat of the above actions unless there is proven
      abstinence
  · a close person turning state's evidence in cases of
      domestic violence or other crime
  · conviction(s) for DUI and/or other crime(s) against
      persons
  · loss of driving or other privileges
  · skyrocketing cost of insurance
  · incarceration
  · loss of income or assets (which may have been used as
      protection from consequences)
  · many other legal, financial or interpersonal problems or
      repercussions

Addicts must often experience massive levels of pain. This may hurt the observer more than the addict, who has anaesthetized himself. The observer is usually shocked that anyone could endure so much, yet not "get it." However, we must allow the pain to work its magic, thus increasing the odds that intervention will result in abstinence. Because thresholds vary greatly from addict to addict, no one can predict how much pain is needed. Therefore, addicts need to be assisted in experiencing consequences in every way possible, short of death or where others may experience serious injury. To increase the odds of permanent recovery, promises of future consequences made in legal and private interventions must be kept.

With recovery, society benefits by replacing a DUI with a sober driver. It also profits by substituting an incompetent, untrustworthy and/or destructive human being with one who may turn out to be extraordinarily talented, productive and faithful. We find that the practicing addict is usually a wonderful and caring person in sobriety. He almost always realizes (eventually) that the pain meted out by consequences was his best friend, and that he has reaped the greatest benefits by becoming sober.

To begin to comprehend this Jekyll and Hyde behavior, we need to explain the action of alcohol on the brain of the addict and how it differs in effect on the non-addict. Since most people who become addicted start with alcohol, this will shed light on the misconduct of those who gravitate toward the "other" drugs as well. Since a drug is a drug to an addict, all substances cause them to engage in destructive behaviors. The existence of addiction should not be confused with the fact that such misconduct and what seem to be Personality Disorders take different forms, depending on the Psychological Type of the addict and the drug(s) he uses.[9] Also, understanding the action of alcohol on the brain is essential if we are to identify the less obvious, yet oftentimes most dangerous on-road misbehaviors in which addicts engage.

1. Anchorage Times, "Our Kids Are Gone," by Karen Aho, July 14, 2000.
2. L.A. Daily News, "Crash Driver Faces Murder Charges," by Amy Collins, December 12, 1997, p. 10.
3. National Highway Safety Traffic Administration, *DWI Detection and Standardized Field Sobriety Testing: Student Manual*, Oklahoma City, OK: U.S. Department of Transportation, October 1995, p. II-4.
4. *DWI Manual*, Ibid.., p. II-4.
5. *DWI Manual,* Ibid., p. II-1
6. *DWI Manual*, Ibid., p. II-2.
7. Booklet, *Alcoholism: A Treatable Disease*, Minneapolis, MI: The Johnson Institute, 1987, p.6. Italics in the original.
8. *DWI Manual*, Ibid., p. II-3.
9. Doug Thorburn, *Using Type and Temperament to Diagnose and Treat Addiction,* Northridge, CA: Galt Publishing, in publication 2002, sheds new light on this role.

1

Alcoholism, Distortions and Brain Damage

Let's clarify a few terms. The words "alcoholism" and "drug addiction" are used interchangeably because alcohol is just one of the many drugs that cause observably destructive behaviors in those susceptible. Because the misconceptions about alcoholism are so rampant, it's important to identify what it is not. Alcoholism is not an uncontrollable desire to drink. This loss of control is characteristic only of latter-stage addicts; those in the early-stages often control their drinking and/or use for extended periods. It is not "having problems in one's life," although this generally occurs eventually. Early-stage addicts often have no more problems than do others due to the fact that over-achievement (a common symptom of early-stage addiction) delays their onset.[1] In addition, parents often protect their young addicted children from consequences, thereby reducing obvious problems. Again, problems permeate the lives of latter-stage addicts to a far greater degree than they do those in the early stages.

We need, instead, a definition that allows for early identification of alcoholism, so that we can *prevent* tragedy rather than being put into a position of always having to react to it. Try this:

Alcoholism is a genetic disorder that causes the afflicted to bio-chemically process alcohol in such a way as to cause him or her to engage in destructive behaviors, at least some of the time.

Before supporting the usefulness of this definition an objection needs to be answered. Some may argue that we shouldn't convict and punish someone for improper conduct resulting from an accident of biology. However, since addiction is the only disease resulting in a change of behavior that causes the afflicted to harm others, it requires the unique treatment of forced acceptance of responsibility and consequences mentioned previously.

The biological processing of alcohol causes brain dysfunction unique to the alcoholic. It impairs the ability of the neo-cortex (the seat of reason and logic) to accurately perceive and judge. The neo-cortex is the "human" part of the brain, capable of learning from experience. While there may also be damage to the lower brain centers responsible for instinctual responses and impulses, these lower centers are set at birth. Therefore, this damage leaves the more primitive parts of the brain (the limbic system) in relatively greater control, causing uncivilized behaviors.

In addition, since this prehistoric part of the brain cannot learn from experience, the addict can't "learn" that he is one. While many addicts may admit to alcoholism in early sobriety or even while still using, they generally don't truly believe that their use causes destructive behaviors and problems. Evidence of this disbelief by addicts can be found at any AA meeting, where a common refrain among recovering addicts is, "Thank God I'm an alcoholic, because when I was using, I wasn't." Addicts long sober often admit that they held to the idea that they were not alcoholics during much of their early recovery.

The other mood altering (psychoactive) drugs also appear to cause brain damage in those predisposed. These include the prescription drugs morphine, codeine, Oxycontin and Vicodin, along with their illegal counterpart, heroin. They include not only legal sedatives, barbiturates and amphetamines, but also Quaaludes, methamphetamine and cocaine. We don't yet fully understand the precise means of early brain damage from drugs other than alcohol, but it's suspected that there may be a similar action. The fact that alcoholics are usually multiple-drug users, almost invariably engaging at some point in destructive behaviors while using, supports this assertion.

The damage to the neo-cortex manifests in bizarre, unethical, criminal and/or psychopathological behaviors in susceptible individuals. In other words:

**Alcoholism causes the afflicted to engage in
destructive behaviors.**

Figure 1 - Chart of Psychoactive Drugs

	Stimulants	CNS Depressants	Narcotics
Legal	caffeine, alcohol*	alcohol*	alcohol*

Legal by Prescription	Adderal
	amphetamines
	Benzedrine
	Dexedrine
	Dextrostat
	Ritalin
		barbiturates:
		  Fiorinal
		  Fioricet
		  Nembutal
		  Seconal
		sedative-hypnotics:
		  Ativan
		  benzodiazepine
		  chloral hydrate
		  Clonazapam (and
		any other "...pam")
		  Dalmane
		  Equinil
		  Halcion
		  Klonopin
		  Librax
		  Librium
		  Miltown
		  Placydil
		  Rostoril
		  Valium
		  Xanax
			opioids:
			  codeine
			  Darvocet
			  Darvon
			  Demerol
			  Dilaudid
			  hydromorphone
			  hydrocordone
			  Lorcet
			  Lortab
			  methadone
			  morphine
			  Tylenol with
			codeine
			  Vicodin
			  Vicodin ES

Illegal	methamphetamine
	Cocaine
		Mathaqualone (quaaludes)	Opiates:
			  Opium
			  Heroin

Note that if there is use without misbehaviors, it's not addiction. Consider the fact that most can drink wine without becoming destructive. On the other hand, a relative few, estimated at about 10% of the population in the U.S., cannot drink this or any other alcoholic beverage without erratically and unpredictably engaging in behaviors that have a negative affect on those around them.

Many attribute this to drinking too much. However, some who drink "too much" do not beat up their spouses, drive under the influence, lie, cheat, steal and/or manipulate others to their own advantage. These "heavy drinkers" often consume less toward middle age. The alcoholic, on the other hand, continues drinking at an alarming rate. He eventually becomes an obvious drunk, a dead one, or in some cases, a recovering alcoholic, which is the goal we hope to advance.

Figure 2
Amundsen's Blood Alcohol Level/Weight Chart[2]

*No. of Drinks	Body Weight in Pounds								
	100	120	140	160	180	200	220	240	
1	0.04	0.03	0.03	0.02	0.02	0.02	0.02	0.02	Not Legally Under
2	0.08	0.06	0.05	0.05	0.04	0.04	0.03	0.03	the Influence
3	0.11	0.09	0.08	0.07	0.06	0.06	0.05	0.05	Driving Ability
4	0.15	0.12	0.11	0.09	0.08	0.08	0.07	0.06	Impaired
5	0.19	0.16	0.13	0.12	0.11	0.09	0.09	0.08	and
6	0.23	0.19	0.16	0.14	0.13	0.11	0.10	0.09	Dangerous
7	0.26	0.22	0.19	0.16	0.15	0.13	0.12	0.11	Definitely Under
8	0.30	0.25	0.21	0.19	0.17	0.15	0.14	0.13	the Influence
9	0.34	0.28	0.24	0.21	0.19	0.17	0.15	0.14	and
10	0.38	0.31	0.27	0.23	0.21	0.19	0.17	0.16	Deadly

HOW TO USE THE CHART

1. *Determine your weight category (use the lower weight if you fall between two categories.)*
2. *Determine the number of drinks you will have, or have, consumed.*
3. *Subtract .015 per cent BAL per hour of drinking*
   Example: A person weighing 160 lbs. drinking six beers in 3 hours would have a BAL level of approximately .09%. This amount is significant and will cause judgment errors. Considered "legally" intoxicated in many states.

* *One "drink" is a 12-ounce bottle of beer, a 5-ounce glass of wine, or 1.5 ounces of 80 proof liquor.*

The reason for this is that alcoholics can drink copious amounts without finding it unpleasant or appearing inebriated, at least to a point. A terrific example of this is Princess Diana's driver, Henri Paul. When I heard that he was driving 90 in a 30-mph zone, I attributed it to alcohol and not to the excuses offered by the media. Those who saw the video of Paul in the hotel prior to this tragic event told me that he appeared completely sober. I responded that driving at such an excessive speed was a strong indication of being under the influence and, if proven to be true, appearing to be sober was a probable confirmation of alcoholism. Three days later, the Blood Alcohol Level (BAL) of Paul was reported at .178 per cent. A 200-pound person would have to drink 13 glasses of wine (two bottles or its equivalent) in a couple of hours to reach this level.

Stories of Paul's fondness for the bottle were reported over subsequent months. A pattern of destructive behavior emerged from various acquaintances, none of who, by themselves, knew the whole story. This is typical of alcoholism, because addicts are like icebergs: 90% of what is really going on lies beneath the surface. This is why, to see the big picture, communication among observers is required. The addict may view this as "conspiracy," but only through such actions can we gain different vantage points to even begin to get an idea of the true extent of the problem.

The single fact that Henri Paul appeared sober when most non-alcoholics would have been visibly plastered clues us into the possibility that he, like all addicts, processes alcohol differently than do non-addicts. It is unusual that non-alcoholics can drink anywhere near as much without showing signs of extreme inebriation. The reason for this biological difference in the processing of the drug may be rooted in a person's ancestry.

Support for this lies in the fact that there is a far greater predisposition to alcoholism among some peoples than others. The suggestion that addiction is due to lack of character carries the implication that some races are innately better in terms of ethics, morality and willpower. On the other hand, a biological difference turns what many consider to be a character flaw or weakness of will into a nonjudgmental genetic disorder. When excess insulin is produced due to an inability to properly process sugar, it's referred to as a disease called diabetes. Since a biological disparity causes addicts to acquire what appear to be behavioral disorders, addiction should also be considered a disease.

Although Southern Europeans have a low risk of alcoholism and their neighbors to the north have a measurably greater risk, there doesn't seem to be any innate differences in character between them. Native Americans, whether living in the desert or polar climates of North America, experience an epidemic rate of alcoholism. We can therefore rule out weather, morality, ethics and character as having a role in the conception of alcoholism.

There *is* a difference in the period of time during which these cultures have had access to large amounts of the fermentable grains used to produce alcohol. It has been hypothesized that access to harvested quantities of such grains for long periods may have created enough alcoholism to build up a resistance. These grains have been available to Southern Europeans for about 10,000-15,000 years, while Northern Europeans have been able to procure such portions for only 1,200 to 1,500 years. The rate of alcoholism is estimated to be three times greater in Northern Europe. Native Americans were introduced to alcohol only 100 to 500 years ago. In terms of micro-evolution, this is zero time to develop resistance to a disease or to allow future generations to otherwise adapt and process a newly introduced chemical in a non- or less harmful way.

How then has the processing of alcohol evolved in such a way that destructive behaviors do not result in some? Both alcoholic and non-alcoholic livers convert this drug into a poison, acetalde-hyde (think: formaldehyde), at equal rates. However, the non-alco-holic is able to quickly process this poison into acetate, a substance that causes nausea and hangover, but is otherwise harmless. This serves as a feedback mechanism that says, "Whoa, slow down!" thus limiting the drinking. Because the alcoholic processes acetaldehyde into acetate much slower, he either does not experi-ence such feedback, or it does not occur until after the BAL has returned to zero. Furthermore, as a result of this slow conversion, there is a buildup of acetaldehyde in the brain of the addict, result-ing in a release of neurotransmitters called isoquinolines, which produce euphoric feelings. Rather than suffering any negative feedback, he experiences a positive one that says "Keep on drink-ing." This combination of feeling great during a drinking episode and not experiencing any ill effects until long after stopping only serves to encourage the addict to continue drinking.

At the same time, the buildup of acetaldehyde causes brain poisoning and cerebral atrophy, measurable in most alcoholics. Since addicts subsequently experience distorted perceptions and non-alcoholics do not, it may be hypothesized that this brain dam-age is the source of distortions.

The specific distortions provide invaluable clues to behaviors in which practicing alcoholics engage. These form the cues by which we can identify possible DUIs and addicts. We will find, however, that many of the most destructive behaviors occur between drinking episodes. This makes sense only if we understand the key distortion, along with short-term withdrawal and the gradual depletion of the body's ability to produce neurotransmitters.

Distortions in perceptions are caused by blackouts, memory repression and euphoric recall. The first two sources of perceptive distortions are not as relevant as the latter to the identification of intoxicated drivers. As observers, we cannot determine whether an alcoholic is experiencing a blackout, which is a period of time when events do not enter into the memory. The addict appears completely aware and sometimes even sober when, in fact, he is stoned and will never remember anything. "Memory repression" causes the addict to suppress memories so shameful or frightening that their recollection could cause him to turn suicidal. (While the human brain does what it can to protect its own, it is not always successful, as evidenced by the number of suicides believed to occur in early recovery.) Again, we cannot determine when the addict is repressing memories. This is especially true from the limited vantage point of another vehicle.

The source of distortions we need to focus on is the one that causes the addict to remember everything he does or says in a self-favoring light. The late alcoholism authority Vernon Johnson referred to this as "euphoric recall."[3] The memory of the alcoholic makes him believe that everything he says or does is good and right and nothing bad or wrong. Since the addict can't be wrong, how can he be blamed for anything? Blame is instead assigned to others. This results in an inability to voluntarily accept responsibility for his transgressions, causing all manners of difficulties for others in all facets of life from the road to the courtroom.

Euphoric recall leads to something even more pernicious: the belief that the addict is godlike. Doing everything right results in an inordinately large sense of self-importance, which is what author James Graham refers to as an "inflated ego." This is the direct cause for what are often the most destructive behaviors exhibited by alcoholics, both during and between drinking episodes.

Physiological impairments from alcohol and other drug use also cause danger. These include a reduced sense of hearing, decreased peripheral vision and slowed reaction time. They account for some of the on-road behaviors and confusion that many falsely believe are the primary dangers resulting from DUIs. We will find that such physical impairments usually pale in comparison with the havoc caused by the alcoholic's inflated ego.

There is another crucial aspect to alcohol and other drug addiction that needs to be understood to make sense of the misbehaviors and mood swings that occur between drinking episodes. A clue may occur when one ponders having had to "walk on eggshells" around a friend, coworker or loved one the morning after a party. This person is almost surely an alcoholic. Think about what his driving behaviors might be like.

This alcoholic, in-between drinking episodes or with a declining Blood Alcohol Level (BAL), is every bit as dangerous, if not more so, as when his BAL is high. He may not lack peripheral vision, his hearing is returning to normal and his reaction time might be greatly improved. However, he may have all the god-like behaviors he had when drinking, along with an even worse attitude. This alcoholic can be observed engaging in some of the most inconsiderate, reckless and dangerous driving behaviors.

This is particularly true for the middle-stage alcoholic, who "*is most sick, not when he drinks, but when he stops drinking.*"[4] This is due to the adaptation to alcohol at the cellular level, in which the cells have become accustomed to functioning with alcohol, accounting for the "smoothed out" drunk. As authors Dr. James R. Milam and Katherine Ketcham put it, "when the alcoholic stops drinking, all hell breaks loose. Blood vessels constrict, cutting down on the flow of blood and oxygen to the cells. The blood glucose level drops sharply and remains unstable...Hormones, enzymes, and body fluid levels fluctuate erratically. The body's cells are malnourished and toxic from long exposure to large doses of alcohol and acetaldehyde."[5] This is why the middle-stage alcoholic is at best, fidgety, anxious and agitated between drinking episodes. At worst, he can become violent.

Since 80-90% of incarcerated prisoners are alcohol and other drug addicts,[6] it may seem puzzling that only half of the criminals apprehended shortly after committing a violent crime have high BALs. The confusion diminishes when we consider that many of the other half are in-between drinks or in BAL decline. Maria Roy, founder and executive director of Abuse Women's Aid in Crisis,

Inc., in studying domestic abusers, reported that 85% of violent husbands had "an alcohol and/or other drug problem." She stated that these men "did not have to be drunk or on other drugs when committing a violent act; *very often, the assaults came during sobriety or when the effects of hard drugs had worn off.*"[7] When we consider the effect of cellular hell breaking loose on the alcoholic without alcohol, it isn't so shocking to find an alcoholic whooping it up at the bar, then going home and beating up his or her spouse. While the BAL is high, he feels good. It is the short-term withdrawal that causes many alcoholics, including those operating motor vehicles, to engage in dramatically destructive behaviors.

Another reason that such behaviors occur between drinks is the gradual depletion of the body's ability to produce "feel good" neurotransmitters on its own. This is especially prominent among poly-drug addicts and those in latter-stage alcoholism, which does not necessarily mean a chronologically older alcoholic. A young person combining numerous drugs for several years may enter latter-stage addiction in his early twenties. An older addict who has spent most of his drinking career bingeing from time to time on only alcohol may never enter this stage.

Two of the depleted neurotransmitters may be responsible for the vast majority of civilized behavior. One, dopamine, increases alertness and feelings of well being. Heavy use of alcohol, cocaine or amphetamines artificially increases levels of dopamine beyond normal quantities. Such use gradually reduces the body's ability to produce this neurotransmitter on its own, resulting in ill feelings and sluggishness when abstinent. The addict high on amphetamines may speed through traffic, performing like a professional racecar driver while increasing risk to everyone in his path. When "coming down" or in-between uses, the collapse in dopamine to levels well below normal may cause him to inflict his wrath on others. The latter situation can be extremely dangerous to anyone who gets in his way.

The other neurotransmitter, serotonin, alleviates depression and increases self-confidence. According to Katherine Ketcham, et al, in *Beyond the Influence,* it also "promotes feelings of well-being, induces sleep, and reduces aggression and compulsive behavior."[8] No wonder the addict, who has depleted his body's ability to produce serotonin, may engage in aggressive and compulsive behaviors between drinking episodes.

The disparate effects on addicts in various stages of their afflic-
tion, as well as with different levels of alcohol or other drugs in
their systems, result in a number of causes that explain their
bizarre actions. All of these behaviors suggest addiction and give
us clues to potentially lethal DUIs and addicts on little or no drugs
at the time. If we know what to look for, we can often see the signs
from another vehicle or from the position of a vulnerable pedestrian long before tragedy strikes. While some of the behaviors may
have several causes, they will be described in one of the following
categories, believed to be their main source:

* A sense of invincibility ("ain't nothin' gonna happen to
    me").
* A Supreme Being complex ("I am God").
* Poor judgment, leading to an increased risk of error.
* Mental confusion.
* Physical signs either of vehicle or person.

Some of the specific signs of DUI described in the following
chapter evolved from personal observation combined with inter-
views of law enforcement officers. Others are found in a National
Highway Traffic Safety Administration (NHTSA) study of nighttime driving behaviors and Blood Alcohol Level (BAL).[9]
According to this study, these clues provide evidence of a high
probability that the driver is legally under the influence. At the
time, this required a BAL of .10 per cent or greater.

It is unfortunate that this study, completed in the mid-1980s,
has not been thoroughly updated. Nor have daytime driving
behaviors been studied. The researchers may have felt that there
would not be enough incidents to warrant a daytime investigation.
On the other hand, due to the lower probability of DUI during
daytime hours, there may have been a lack of cases and a resulting
inability to find accurate results. Or, they may have simply not rec-
ognized that there are some addicts who wake up to a morning
"eye opener" containing several ounces of 80-proof liquor mixed
in with their breakfast juice. If such a study were to be conducted
on weekend days, there might be enough DUI arrests to provide
meaningful statistics. Until this is done, it may be safe to assume
that daytime clues are at least similar in importance to those devel-

oped from the nighttime study. So, in what follows we do not distinguish between day and night.

The estimates for the clues that were found in the NHTSA study providing a high probability of DUI are shown below in parentheses immediately after the specific behavior. The vast majority of these will be found in categories 3 and 4, "Poor Judgment" and "Mental Confusion." The reasons will become apparent when considering the effect of the key distortion, euphoric recall, on ego-inflation even while not drinking, as well as the effect of brain chemistry on the addict in short-term withdrawal and in-between drinking episodes. The estimates mean that when this behavior was observed, the driver was DUI that part of the time. For example, "Almost striking an object, vehicle or person (60%)" means that in 60 out of 100 cases in which this behavior was observed, the driver had a BAL of .10 per cent or higher. Note that the likelihood of the driver's BAL exceeding .08 per cent (the new federal government limit) would no doubt be greater. The probabilies that the BAL is higher than .04 per cent are even larger. This is the point at which reckless behaviors begin in the addict and reaction times are reduced in everyone.

The *DWI Detection and Standardized Field Sobriety Testing: Student Manual*, in which the study results are described, suggests that if multiple behaviors are observed, 10% should be added to the higher value. For example, if a person is seen "almost striking an object, vehicle or person" and is also viewed "drifting," for which probabilites of DUI were found to be 60% and 50% respectively, 10% should be added to the larger value. So, when both "almost striking" and "drifting" are observed, we add 10% to the higher probability clue, giving a 70% chance of DUI. It may be suggested that if any one clue is repeated, the same system can be applied (adding 10% for each instance) until 100% probability is reached.

Now, in real life we can rarely prove a 100% likelihood that someone is an alcohol or other drug addict. However, if one is DUI, the shift in attitudes since 1980 has made the chances of addiction extremely high.

1. James Graham, in *The Secret History of Alcoholism*, Rockport, MA: Element Books, Inc., 1996, identified over-achievement as a common by-product of "ego inflation." By no means should it be construed that all over-achievers are addicts, any more than are all smokers.

2. Everett R. Amundsen, *National Responsible Drivers* handbook, p. 26.

3. Vernon E. Johnson, *I'll Quit Tomorrow*, San Francisco, CA: Harper and Row, 1980.

4. Dr. James R. Milam and Katherine Ketcham, *Under the Influence: A Guide to the Myths and Realities of Alcoholism*, New York: Bantam Books, 1983, p. 64. Italics in the original.

5. Milam and Ketcham, Ibid., p. 65.

6. Doug Thorburn, *Drunks, Drugs & Debits*, Northridge, CA: Galt Publishing, 2000, pp. 13-16, makes a compelling case for this.

7. . Maria Roy, Ed., *Battered Women: A Psychosociological Study of Domestic Violence*, New York: Van Nostrand, 1977, p. 39. Emphasis added.

8. Katherine Ketcham, et al, *Beyond the Influence: Understanding and Defeating Alcoholism*, New York: Bantam Books, 2000, p. 81.

9. Reported in *DWI Manual*, Ibid., pp. V-3 through V-8.

2

A Sense of Invincibility

While this behavior is common among young people, it's even more so among young alcoholics regardless of BAL. Authors Katherine Ketcham and James Milam point out in their book, *Under the Influence*, that the early-stage alcoholic is extraordinarily functional. During this stage, he actually performs better while under the influence at a far higher BAL than is commonly thought possible. This adds to his feeling of invincibility and takes form in very obvious, reckless behaviors. We've never been taught to think that alcoholism might be the main cause of such behaviors, yet it should be the primary suspect.

We should bear in mind that a person may not be under the influence when such destructive behaviors occur. If a suspect is pulled over or involved in an accident, it shouldn't be a surprise if he initially passes the officer's tests. However, the officer should take a closer look at his pupils and overall behavior. If there is any suspicion of being under the influence based on pupil size, lack of response to light, or his overall excitability and irritability, a Drug Recognition Expert should be summoned. This is someone in law enforcement with special training in the identification of the drug or drugs a person has in his system. Less than 20% of all police officers nationwide have had this training. Even if there is no alcohol, the suspect may test positive for amphetamines, cocaine or other substances. Discussions with recovering addicts confirm that the following behaviors were common among them in active addiction, even when not under the influence. These are signs and symptoms of a sense of invincibility that normally result only from addiction.

1. Speeding recklessly through traffic.

Believing that everything he does is right (remember euphoric recall), leads to a sense that he can do no wrong. This feeds his feeling of invincibility. Why not speed in a crazy manner? After all, even if an accident actually occurs, he won't get hurt (never mind anyone else involved).

There's something else at work here as well, which may put many of those who speed recklessly in the next category, the Supreme Being complex. Addiction expert Harry M. Tiebout, M.D. in his 1954 pamphlet, "The Ego Factors in Surrender to Alcoholism," was among the first to explain the inordinately large sense of self-importance, called "inflated ego," observable in alcoholics. He distinguished this from Sigmund Freud's ego (a personality aspect between id and superego) yet integrated this inflated self-view with Freud's observations regarding infants. Tiebout pointed out that the alcoholic ego emanates from three infantile factors. One is the infant's psyche, summarized in Freud's brilliant summation, "His Majesty, the Baby." The infant "is born ruler of all he surveys." This is omnipotence proffering special rights, privileges and positions, as if godlike.

The second is derived from the observation that infants tolerate frustration poorly and let the world know it since, in Tiebout's words, "One of the prerogatives of royalty is to proceed without interruption." This leads to an imperious attitude on the part of the grown addict and a belief that he is unstoppable, which results in the feeling of invincibility.

The third trait left over from infancy is the tendency to do everything in a hurried state, thinking, talking, moving and living faster, like the toddler running to see his grandparents. This would explain the alcoholic often being in a hurry, more so than the average person. It could also account for the big plans, hopes, promises and schemes that, while often matched with an ability to accomplish in early-stage addiction, are unmatched in the latter stage. This tendency combined with the expectation of being able to proceed without interruption can account for the addict's propensity to speed through traffic, whether or not he is under the influence.

Regardless of the behavior's source, this person is potentially lethal. We need to get out of his way and he needs to be apprehended, for his own sake as well as ours.

2. Not wearing a seat belt.

The idea of invincibility increases the odds of not protecting oneself, even when it's so easy to do. This is particularly true in the case of seat belts, which have been repeatedly proven to save lives and decrease the extent of injury in almost every kind of accident.

It's difficult for the non-addict seat belt user to fathom not buckling up. Yet, many recovering addicts report that they rarely used seat belts. Before the advent of mandatory seat belt use and even today where use is either voluntary or not adhered to on a large scale, this is not a good clue. But where vigorously enforced, it may be a terrific one.

Another reason for not using seat belts is that addicts inflate their egos by flouting the law. The addict often believes that rules do not pertain to him and he doesn't need to obey them. Like Freud's infant, he's been given "special rights." This excuse falls under the heading Supreme Being complex, but is believed to be of secondary importance for not complying with this simple safety mandate.

As with every clue, there are exceptions to the rule. For example, I know of one person, for whom there are no other signs of addiction, who never uses a seat belt. He was involved in an accident in which he was the only person not wearing one and the only survivor. He was thrown free of the car before it rolled down a steep embankment, killing the driver and other passenger. The strict logicians among us may disagree with his conclusions, but we can't argue with his feelings and what he believes to be his "karma."

3. Doing several things at once ("multi-tasking"), such as driving, putting on make-up, reading the paper, eating, smoking, changing radio stations and using a mobile phone.

Since the addict is always in a hurry, he will often attempt to do many things at the same time. Behaviors that have the earmark of a sense of invincibility are especially common in the high-strung amphetamine or cocaine addict, who may or may not have any alcohol in his system. The higher the blood alcohol level, the less capable he is of successfully multi-tasking without incident. However, there is some evidence that with a quantity of "uppers" in his system, he may be able to multi-task at a very high BAL. Some recovering addicts report that they could keep on drinking and functioning for extended periods with these drugs coursing through their veins.

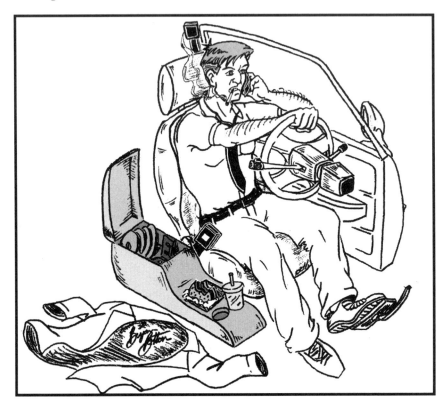

4. On a mobile phone and either attempting to do anything else and/or engaging in any degree of reckless driving behavior.

It is commonly believed that using a mobile phone is more dangerous than engaging in other tasks while driving. Studies that report such use resulting in accident rates equal to those of DUIs may be measuring the wrong thing. If the study doesn't test for alcohol and other drugs in blood and urine, there is little chance that the casual observer would find any. The Florida study in which police officers detected only 22% of the DUI violators they investigated, supports the assertion that many addicts do not exhibit obvious signs of inebriation to BALs as high as .24 per cent. Therefore, we must look to behaviors rather than superficial appearances to determine the likelihood of addiction or DUI.

Unnecessarily heavy phone use is, in itself, one behavioral clue to alcoholism. This is especially true when very drunk or causing the other party inconvenience, for example by calling late at night. Recall that addicts inflate their ego by exerting control over others. By keeping the other person listening, the alcoholic puts himself in a "one-up" position. Therefore, observing someone using a mobile phone may give us a slight advantage in identifying likely addicts. This is particularly true if such use occurs when it may be dangerous, as in heavy stop-and-go traffic, poor weather conditions, or while speeding. When in conjunction with driving and attempting to multi-task (as in the previous clue) or engaging in any reckless behaviors, we may well be observing an addict…whether or not he is DUI.

On the opposite side of the fence, the non-addict is likely to become even more careful when driving and using a mobile phone. I often call my office for messages or 911 emergency to report errant drivers. However, I'm especially careful to follow every law and safe driving practice when doing so. This no doubt applies to most other non-addict drivers.

5. Speeding up to make the light after it's turned red.

As we have seen, the alcoholic is always in a hurry and thinks that he should be able to "proceed without interruption." This hurried state may account, in part, for the fact that the person running a red light in this manner may be an overachiever, perhaps a talented sports/screen star, CEO of a major corporation or politician. Since he may be unable to run out of the money that protects him from consequences he so desperately needs, being apprehended for DUI or other legal infraction is the next best thing. Numerous tickets on his record can greatly increase the odds of successful intervention by family, employer and/or the judicial system.

What is "enough" varies by addict. For some, it's one arrest, while for others dozens are too few. However, intervention dramatically improves the odds that the latest arrest will result in sobriety.

6. Markedly speeding up, crossing a yellow light and barely making it.

Again, the addict is always rushing, like the toddler running for the big red ball. Some of us occasionally do this, but the addict, if this is his particular style, may do so repeatedly.

It's important to understand that the behaviors of addicts take various forms. Many yell and scream but never hit anyone, while others maim and even kill. Some addicts pour on "alcoholic charm" to get what they want, others merely intimidate. Some belittle and even falsely accuse spouses of cheating, all the while committing adultery themselves. Still others are loyal to their spouses, yet embezzle funds and commit larceny at work.

The same is true for driving behaviors. Some don't drive over the speed limit and wear a seat belt, while others speed, tailgate, never wear a seat belt and talk incessantly on mobile phones. Many addicts live their entire lives without getting so much as a traffic violation, while a few make the news due to a 12th arrest for DUI. The fact is, styles of addiction vary greatly. We need to be alert to the idea that if any serially destructive behavior is observed on or off the road, addiction should be suspected.

7. Speeding up to make a left turn in front of someone with inadequate distance.

Making a left turn in front of someone could fit in several of these categories, including "poor judgment" or "mental confusion." He really could be thinking, "I have plenty of time," or, "The driver in the opposing lane of traffic will slow down enough to let me through." If done in a high-speed style, it could be due to the Supreme Being complex. However in most cases, this just shows a sense of invincibility.

It is unfortunate that the person in front of whom the turn was made will generally not have an opportunity to report the culprit. However, there is another potential victim who may be able to do so: the driver making a left turn immediately behind the possible addict. If an accident occurs, this person may well become involved, if only because of skidding and colliding vehicles right in front of him. I had occasion to report one of these, as we were both turning into a shopping center. Parking in a position to observe, I watched her fumble inside her SUV for a minute or two, stagger into a restaurant, return to her vehicle with a take-out order and drive off. Unfortunately, as so often occurs, the police did not show up in time to stop her.

8. Turning with excessive speed (35% probability of DUI according to the NHTSA study).

This can be very dangerous in SUVs, some of which are known to roll over easily. The sober driver knows this, so he typically won't do it. However, the DUI, or even the addict in-between uses, may well do so because, as he will tell us, "I know what I'm doing. I'm a great driver. I am invincible." He may be an excellent driver, especially in early-stage alcoholism. That doesn't mean he's not wreaking havoc in his home life or causing others to have serious accidents because he puts them in jeopardy by driving recklessly or engaging in other at-risk behaviors.

9. Tailgating (50% probability), while not trying too hard to get around traffic.

These tailgaters probably think that they can brake quickly enough if the person in front stops suddenly. This feeling may stem from a sense of invincibility (it won't happen to me) or simply from poor judgment. We will find that the potentially more lethal kind is the "Supreme Being" complex type of tailgating discussed later.

10. Excessive speed with a child in the vehicle.

This may be a result of poor judgment or "I am invincible." In either case, this person needs to be arrested.

Interestingly, "excessive speed" in itself is not one of the clues found to be an indication of DUI in the NHTSA study. While it's likely that many of the additional clues discussed were not thought up or considered too rare to provide meaningful statistics, one would think that this is not true for speeding. However, when too many people engage in a particular behavior, it negates its value as a clue either to DUI or addiction. Smoking where everyone does it, as in Japan, is an example of such behavior. For most parts of the United States, it's speeding. However, speeding with a child may be a terrific clue because most people tend to be extra-cautious when driving with children. Not even this will get the alcohol-addict to drive more conservatively, especially if under the influence.

When tempted to think, "No, my addict would never do such a thing!" consider the fact that addicts are responsible for 85% of domestic violence. Such abuse is committed against people who, by definition, are personally and often intimately known. Addicts are usually wonderful, caring and concerned people when in a program of sobriety. The early-stage addict excels at being charming, witty and extremely careful not to offend those whom he wishes to lure into personal, financial or professional relationships. However, just like Robert De Niro's character in the Tobias Woolf autobiography, *This Boys' Life*, once he has what he wants, all hell can—and often does—break loose. If addicts engage in violence against those whom in their right minds they would love, they wouldn't think twice about driving under the influence with children in the vehicle.

A study conducted in June, 2000 by the Ford Motor Co. and the University of Michigan Transportation Research Institute supports this assertion. It reported that "more than half of elementary school-aged children killed in alcohol-related crashes were not with a drunken teenager," but were instead, being driven by a person "of parent age who was intoxicated."[1]

11. Speeding at 25 mph or more over the speed limit.

As previously mentioned, this isn't listed in the DRE manual as being indicative of DUI. However, at some excessive speeds, even without traffic, there is an increased likelihood of being under the influence. While not endangering others if there is no traffic nearby, at some point a person takes his life into his hands. Many perfectly healthy non-addicts do this, including racecar drivers, rock climbers and extreme skiers. However, there are recovering addicts who inform us that they climbed cliffs, skied down near-vertical slopes and drove at speeds in excess of 100 mph when nobody else was around. They often don't engage in these behaviors when drinking; if they did, addicts would have a life expectancy even shorter than the 14 years by which their average life span is already reduced.

Speeding in isolated areas isn't, by itself, as risky a behavior as speeding through traffic. Studies have found that speed differentials are far more dangerous than simply speeding. For example, weaving through traffic at 10 mph faster than other vehicles is probably more dangerous than driving at 30 mph above the speed limit on a deserted highway. On the other hand, exceeding the limit by 15 mph in the slow lane of a residential street with parked cars and a risk of children or pets suddenly appearing, is quite dangerous for everyone concerned.

12. Passing on a two-lane highway over a solid yellow line.

This is potentially so dangerous that it is rare, but many have seen it done once or twice in their driving career. Unnecessary acts that could be lethal and which violate the rights of others, are almost exclusively the province of addicts. This one should be no exception.

13. Passing quickly to the left before the official left-hand turn lane.

While this may be due to impaired judgment, there is a certain sense of invincibility whispering to the addict that no one in front will decide to turn left at the same time. If they do, it's the other guy's fault anyway, right?

Once, while making a turn into a left turn lane, I almost collided with a van speeding past me in that lane. The female driver had come from behind, entering before the opening (in the double-double yellow zone preceding it). For research purposes, I decided to follow her. As she stopped in front of an elementary school, a child boarded. I crept up next to her and, rolling down the window, asked if she realized whether I had almost run into her. She answered with an obscenity. As we will find, that alone strongly supported a hypothesis of DUI or addiction. This was one of several incidents providing inspiration to obtain a mobile phone. Today, I would report her in an instant for likely DUI, especially with a child as a passenger.

Some may cringe that I would willingly see a parent arrested in front of a child, with possible loss of custody as a consequence. Yet, it can be reasonably assumed that such a child has already experienced all manners of problems, including hearing obscenities such as the one said to me. We adults know that the darkest hour comes just before the dawn. This is an instance where judicial intervention may be extremely productive and where close persons can educate the child, gently explaining that mommy has a disease causing her to act in ways unlike her real self. The only way by which to create a better parent is to help her suffer consequences and crises. We must always keep in mind that the goal is to do whatever is necessary to increase the likelihood of successful intervention. Many recovering female addicts report that the only thing that finally forced them to make a decision to get clean and sober was the threat or actual loss of custody of a child.

14. Excessive speed in inclement weather, including fog, snow or ice.

One of the scariest drives I've ever taken was one December on Interstate 5 through California's Central Valley. I suddenly hit a fog bank in which I could barely see 10 feet ahead. Slowing from 70 to 35 mph wasn't enough for me, yet I feared being hit from behind if I decelerated any further. As it was, others passed me as if I were standing still.

This probably emanates from an "I am invincible" attitude, often in conjunction with a bit of our next category, the Supreme Being complex. Many were driving SUVs. If there had been an accident, they probably felt they wouldn't have been as badly injured as those in sedans.

Figure 3 -- Average Stopping Distances Under Different Conditions[2]

Condition	Feet to stop at various miles per hour				
	20 mph	30 mph	40 mph	50 mph	60 mph
Dry Concrete	47	88	149	243	366
Gravel	70	135	232	374	561
Wet Pavement	78	147	252	404	607
Packed Snow	105	194	336	541	808
Ice or Sleet	235	430	745	1215	1830

1. Melanie Axelrod, *ABCnews.com*, June 20, 2000.
2. Adapted from Amundson, Ibid., p. 42.

3

A Supreme Being Complex ("I am God")

This is caused by the key distorted self-perception earlier referred to as euphoric recall, compelling the addict to view everything in a self-favoring way. Rather than being intentional, it is a result of brain poisoning that is caused by a buildup of acetaldehyde occurring only in addicts.

The truly insidious aspect is that the addict thinks he can do no wrong. Believing he does everything right over and over creates a reinforcing pattern in his damaged brain. He eventually thinks he is on par with God. The evidence from the trial of Susan Conkey Rhea suggests that she seems to have held this belief. Driving home from a bar with a blood alcohol level of almost .24 per cent, she plowed into Jesus Berumen's compact car at 80 mph as he sat at a red light. She was reported to have sat in her crumpled car, looking into her lighted vanity mirror wiping her face, while several yards away Berumen could be heard screaming as he incinerated in his car. Police testified that at the hospital emergency room she cockily told them, "You can't touch me. You can't arrest me. I'm a stockbroker. My attorney is Harland Braun. I'll never go to jail."[1] She may as well have said, "I am God." No doubt, she had managed to stay out of jail several times before despite past arrests and convictions for drunk driving.

The inordinately large sense of self-importance explains addicts' behaviors ranging from simple belittling remarks to the cult of personality that some build with huge support among the well-meaning and credulous. This includes amphetamine addicts such as Adolf Hitler, who had huge support around the world during most of the 1930s,[2] and Jim Jones, who led 900 men, women and children to a mass suicide in Jonestown, Guyana in 1978.[3] It also includes alcoholics such as Joseph Stalin, called the "Supreme Alcoholic" by writer James Graham, who had such extraordinary support that he was able to get away with murdering 25-50 million Soviet citizens.[4] The following driving behaviors are believed to originate from this complex.

1. Tailgating (50% probability), while speeding and obviously trying to get through traffic.

This is my biggest pet peeve. I often tap my brakes in quick succession three times to let the driver behind me know that he is following too close. If he backs off, he may have simply not been paying attention. Or, he may have been displaying a sense of invincibility. However, if he doesn't back off, he likely thinks that he's God. The latter is obviously more threatening.

Someone with such a gargantuan sense of self-importance could be extremely dangerous, even if not DUI. On the other hand, he may be mixing booze with amphetamines or cocaine, or just be doped up on speed. In any event, this is not a person to fool with. Get out of the way and, as he passes, take down his license plate number. He should be immediately reported for reckless endangerment of others and possible DUI.

For the visually gifted, this is a terrific opportunity to notice whether the suspect is wearing a seat belt or shows any other physical signs of DUI, such as smoking or other multi-tasking. When calling 911, it might be helpful if you inform them that the DRE manual suggests a 50% chance of DUI if tailgating. Any other visual clues should be mentioned. These added facts allow the police to give a sobriety test regardless of whether officers witness any of these behaviors. As always, be prepared to provide the exact location. This is a situation where, if other clues are evident (especially if a child is in the car), you might ask to remain on the line until the person is apprehended.

2. Obscene gestures (60%).

The very high probability of DUI found in the NHTSA study is consistent with the observation that alcoholics and their children often utter excessive profanities. As a child of an alcoholic father, I grew up regularly hearing such language and not only became accustomed to it, but also colored my own speech with such obscenities for many years. The number of comedians who are known alcoholics and use this kind of language in their acts is legendary. Such speech is a great clue to addiction in or near the person.

In discussing driving behaviors, obviously one making such gestures is doing so to a person unknown. Since he doesn't know how the recipient may react, this could be dangerous to him and therefore may be a sign of invincibility. However, it more likely falls under the Supreme Being classification because these hand signals are intended to be derogatory. Insulting others through belittling, disparaging remarks, sarcasm, obscenities or obscene gestures results from a sense that one is self-righteous. He is saying that others do (and are) wrong. This is a classic sign of an inflated ego, suggestive of drug addiction. As with most clues, these behaviors may occur during periods of momentary sobriety when the addict can be every bit as dangerous as when using.

3. Road rage.

A study of disruptive airline passengers leading to pilot errors reported that 43% of such incidents were directly related to excessive alcohol consumption.[5] An additional 8% were on (other) drugs or prescription medications, which can be assumed to be psychotropic drugs like Valium and Vicodin. Therefore, the majority of the unruly passengers were under the influence of something. Since these people created havoc at a time when it was extremely dangerous to do so, they engaged in destructive behaviors and are, by our definition, identifiable addicts. Another 9% of such incidents were linked to passengers smoking in lavatories. Since 90% of alcoholics smoke and these smokers were engaging in their habit when forbidden and potentially dangerous, they also exhibited classic symptoms of alcoholism.

Another 15% involved fighting over use of prohibited electronic devices and 5% were bomb or hijack threats. Since there is, as we have seen, a high likelihood that virtually all of these potentially destructive incidents involve an addict (intoxicated or not), we're up to 80% of these events involving likely addicts. Half, if not the entire remaining 20% labeled as "other," could still involve addicts. A reasonable guess, then, as to the percentage of such cases involving addicts is 75% to nearly 100%.

Why would road rage be any different than its in-the-sky equivalent? While 100% of those involved in aircraft disturbances are investigated, relatively few of those exhibiting rage while driving are even apprehended much less tested. A number of Drug Recognition Experts believe that alcohol plays a significant, probably vastly under-recognized role in this. This should not be surprising, at least to us.

4. Cutting a tight corner combined with speeding during a left turn.

Picture yourself waiting to make a left turn at a red light in a legal position behind a crosswalk, facing north. Someone on the cross street comes tearing by you from your right (from the east, heading west), turning left (south), cutting the corner within inches of your front bumper. Because you can clearly see his face as he moves to your left, you may note that this probably isn't a sloppy drunk and that cutting such a tight corner is not likely a result of poor judgment or mental confusion. While it may be a sign of invincibility, if there is an accident it probably won't result in serious injury to him. My suspicion is that these are likely highly functional "get out my way" types who fall under the Supreme Being category. Too bad we're not usually in a position to take down the license plate. However, a law enforcement officer witnessing this behavior may have reasonable grounds to at least make a stop. In a perfect world, a quick sobriety check would be performed on anyone pulled over.

5. Not yielding the right-of-way (45%), especially with an attitude.

One form of this behavior may be observed at intersections with 4-way stop or "yield" signs. Once again, "His Majesty, the Baby" feels he should be allowed to proceed first. The most common form of this is "cutting in line," worthy of its own discussion.

6. Cutting in line.

The infantile trait of always being in a hurry described by Dr. Tiebout is at the root of this behavior. It originates in the child-like ego and, in addicts, grows into an inflated one by young adulthood. Most people, seeing that traffic is backed up onto a freeway transition road a mile ahead (in the L.A. area, one thinks of the 405 northbound transition to the 101) move to that lane and patiently wait their turn. Or, when seeing a large lighted construction arrow indicating a closed lane ahead, normal people begin moving over immediately. Addicts don't do this, since that would place them in a position of equality with everyone else. If one were "king," he would naturally butt in front of his subjects. He would merge into the proper lane only at the last possible second.

For those who don't live in cities, transition lanes may need some explaining. These are often gridlocked, while the "through" lanes are moving at 45-60 mph. The driver forcing his way in at the last possible moment slows traffic in a free-moving lane, sometimes even coming to a complete stop with the rear of his vehicle sticking out. Due to the presumption in the law that the person crashing into another from behind is guilty, this is particularly dangerous to the financial well being of others, even those several cars behind as they come to a screeching halt. Often, the culprit causes an accident without being part of it.

Like many others, this clue doesn't require that one be DUI at the time the transgression occurs. Addicts, whether or not under the influence, are far more likely to engage in such rude and often potentially dangerous behaviors than are non-addicts. Because of the greatly increased risk of getting rammed from behind, this maneuver may also be a sign of the addict's sense of invincibility.

Although non-addicts engage in such behavior, it is probably far more common among those addicted. Where the line-up can't be seen from far behind, it does not serve as a clue to DUI or addiction. When the backup can be seen it is probably an excellent clue, especially if the stunt is particularly dangerous. This would include times when there are substantial speed differentials between the merging and "through traffic" lanes. It's probably a great clue when the driver is also engaging in multi-tasking, in-car behaviors.

Some may protest that since this and other clues presented haven't been studied, they are only hypotheses. However, given the logic involved and the correlations with behaviors that have been tested, most of these should prove valid. If a few don't turn out as expected, that's ok. Regardless of whether or not addiction is behind potentially dangerous behaviors, we need to be extra cautious when near such persons. Law enforcement officers should be ticketing these drivers and giving them sobriety tests whenever possible. This is very different from our private lives, where we must hide the fact that we are scrutinizing a close person for possible addiction.[6] On the road, we aren't trying to confirm addiction. Here, we want to let the addict know that he is being watched, since a greater threat of being caught DUI may inspire one to try sobriety.

7. Passing to the right in a right-hand turn lane, without turning right.

This move, called "snaking," is very similar to "cutting in line." Here, we have the same godlike behavior, rooted in an infantile attitude that results in an expectation of being able to "proceed without interruption." When observed, it is a terrific sign of an imperious attitude. In my experience, this behavior has, on every occasion, coincided with several other clues to DUI or addiction.

8. Littering.

Practicing alcoholics are relatively unconcerned with harming the property of others. In fact, addicts are probably the consummate anti-environmentalists regardless of professed belief. Tossing a cigarette butt or any other litter out the window is an excellent clue to the "I don't care about you" attitude created by the effect of the chemical on the brain of the addict.

A related observation supporting this concept is the trashing of rented homes. There is much evidence to support the idea that almost all "tenants from hell" are also addicts. In my tax practice, I have deducted thousands of dollars in cleanup and repair costs on the tax returns of a number of hapless landlords due to tenant vandalism. In virtually every one of these cases, the addict connection was made. Although most environmentalists may not be addicts, I am aware of one situation in which members of a large international organization normally concerned with protecting the environment rented a condominium in the resort of Mammoth Lakes, California for a weekend. They were reported by a very upset guest in the complex to have been drinking heavily and using foul language in front of his children in the common area spa. I later learned that they were responsible for $2,000 in damage to the condominium they had rented. As practicing addicts, even environmentalists can be extremely anti-environmental (in the broad sense of the term) when it comes to their private lives.

If littering from a car is observed, begin watching for other behaviors suggestive of DUI. Usually, I like to see three or more clues (either the same or different) before dialing 911. When it comes to littering, all I need is one more.

9. Windows tinted to the point where we can't see the driver's face.

"I am God, so I get to see you but you can't be allowed to see me." Kind of reminds one of the Wizard of Oz. A pompous view of self-importance with no self-esteem may strike a chord. This observation began as a hunch; observing the driving behaviors of those with such glass has led me to believe that it may be a correct one. In addition, it is illegal to obscure glass beyond a certain point, yet it is done all the time by those willing to flout the law. After all, as far as the addict is concerned, laws are only for the "other" guy.

10. Driving alone in a lane requiring at least two people.

This is classic "Supreme Being" behavior. A sense of invincibility is also apparent because a person breaking this rule risks a very expensive fine ($271 in California). Unfortunately, he generally gets away with it.

Even those of us who do not support these "diamond" lanes probably don't violate the rules. Recovering alcoholics admit that "the rules were not for me" was a common refrain when they were drinking.

11. Parking in a handicapped space without a placard or disability.

This is another set of rules with which one may reasonably disagree even while following. Some may object to government intervention requiring that private businesses set aside portions of their property for specific groups. However, most of us follow the law, like it or not. Addicts are far more likely to play the game of "sociopathic rule-breaker."

I once glared at an obviously healthy person who parked in a handicapped zone without a placard. My look wasn't so much, "you nasty man you." It was more like, "I come to this lot every other day and I abide by the rules; why can't you?" Okay, a bit of envy, I suppose. It was interesting that (with his hands visible) he came up to the passenger side of my car and asked me what my problem was, as he squished his face against the glass. I realized that his problem was the problem of addiction and did not respond. You may want to think twice before staring.

12. Unnecessarily taking up two parking spaces.

A vehicle unnecessarily taking up two slots is a sign that the vehicle's owner may have an inordinately large sense of self-importance. This, as we have seen, is evidence of possible alcoholism. Recalling that we cannot predict how or when the destructive behaviors of a practicing addict may occur, we can surmise that making contact with this person may be dangerous and even fatal.

There was no parking available when Stephen Wells, 36 and his nephew Jerry Rios, Jr., 11 drove into California's Morro Strand State Beach Campground on July 9, 2001. However, one truck was taking up two spots. Wells had his nephew go ask the owner if he wouldn't mind moving his vehicle to make room for one more. This turned out to be a tragic mistake. After cursing at the young boy, the man, Stephen A. Deflaun, shot and killed both Wells and his nephew before Deflaun himself was shot and wounded by a park ranger. Considering the amount of alcoholic drinking going on in parks, it may be surprising that this was only the sixth time in California State Park history that a ranger had to use his gun. This was just one of thousands of tragedies occurring every day that might have been averted.

After reading about this incident, I asked several non-alcoholic owners of large SUVs or very nice new cars about taking up two spaces. They said they sometimes did this, but only in the far corners of lots. I then asked whether they would take up two spaces if a lot was full. All replied that they would not.

From my own experience, I was trying to park one evening many years ago in a movie theater parking area. There was only one free space around. Unfortunately, the vehicle next to it was two feet over the parking stall line. At the time I was driving a small Volkswagen and managed to carefully squeeze in. I later came out of the movie theater to find the other car gone and mine vandalized with key marks from front to back. Because of my research on alcoholism, I now suspect that this person likely had this disease, as do many who unnecessarily take up two parking spaces.

13. Evading tolls at a tollbooth.

The addict, always in a hurry, "deserves" special rights and privileges. These include being allowed to proceed without interruption and not compensating others for services such as roads. This is yet another way by which the addict wields power over others. Even though relatively non-destructive in itself, it should put us on alert that there may be far more going on with this person than the casual unsuspecting observer will find.

This may have been the case for Wesley Ridgwell of Florida. He was photographed 705 times between August 1999 and June 2000 zipping through tollbooths with a vanity plate reading "JST CRZY". After finally being stopped and facing a $15,000 fine, he was reported to have responded, "I'm such a good person. People who know me just can't believe this is happening." He claims that someone stole his license plate and put it on a car similar to his. However, he couldn't explain his dozen convictions for speeding and drunk driving.[7]

To protect those we care about (including ourselves) we should never underestimate the outlandish gall and nerve of likely addicts, or the number and form of transgressions for which they may be guilty.

1. Jeanette DeSantis, *L.A. Daily News*, "Motorist convicted in DUI death," July 31, 1996, p. 3.
2. Heston, Leonard L., M.D., and Renate Heston, R.N., *The Medical Casebook of Adolf Hitler*, New York: Stein and Day, 1980.
3. Wooden, Kenneth, *The Children of Jonestown, New York:* McGraw-Hill Book Company, 1981.
4. Graham, Ibid., pp. 155-187.
5. NASA study, reported in USA Today, June 12, 2000.
6. . A detailed discussion of this can be found in Thorburn, *Drunks, Drugs & Debits,* Ibid. and Graham, Ibid.
7. *L.A. Daily News,* "Toll evader denies everything," November 26, 2000.

4

Poor Judgment, Leading to Increased Risk of Driver Error

These are the clues most often found by the NHTSA study to be indicative of DUI. They are not rooted in an inflated ego, but are instead simply indications of drunkenness. These include driving behaviors of an early-stage alcoholic with a very high BAL or a latter-stage one with a more moderate blood level. They could even be attributed to a non-addict who is less than or barely over the legal limit. However, this is unusual since non-addicts rarely drive after becoming inebriated.

The threshold over which somebody is legally intoxicated is a presumptive one. If exceeded, the driver is assumed to be drunk. If below this level, the burden of proof falls on the authorities. Paradoxically, officers have a far easier case against non-alcoholics, who may slur their words and stagger at BALs as low as .05 per cent. On the other hand, the highly tolerant early-stage alcoholic may not show the "normal" signs of inebriation until well over .20 per cent. This is the reason why a DUI is not a sure sign of alcoholism: the non-alcoholic is probably far more likely to be apprehended per mile driven while inebriated than is the addict. However, the addict is still more likely to be arrested for DUI because he drives under the influence so much more often than does the non-addict. Of course after his arrest a non-alcoholic will probably never again drive while intoxicated, but the addict will.

The likelihood of DUI that the NHTSA found may seem surprisingly high for some of these clues, especially as stand-alone probabilities. Why, then, have some been proven to strongly suggest DUI and others that logically should be included have not? Some have probably not been studied. If we had the ability to con-

firm, we might find that many of these indications could be common to alcoholics suffering the effects of brain poisoning in-
between drinking episodes. Others might yield a BAL between .04
and .08 per cent, a level at which reckless behaviors in alcoholics
often begin. Possible candidates for zero to low BALs may be
addicts who litter, cut in line and speed while using a mobile
phone.

1. Almost striking an object, vehicle or person (60%).
The cause of this can be traced to three different categories:
invincibility, which leads an addict to believe that he is capable of
doing several things at once; Supreme Being complex, which
includes the behavior of cutting tight corners; and poor judgment,
common among those who lack peripheral vision or depth perception due to inebriation.

2. Actually striking an object, vehicle or person.
Amazingly, the NHTSA employee with whom I spoke during
my research said that the likelihood of DUI in non-injury accidents
is a paltry 7%. I pointed to their own finding that if someone
almost struck an object, vehicle or person, the likelihood of DUI is
60%. I asked him how a near miss to an accident would yield such
a high probability while an actual one would only be a fraction of
this figure. He couldn't answer. I was also informed that this clue
had not been studied directly and that the estimate was calculated
based on other factors that he couldn't identify.

Studies of other kinds of accidents and the role of alcohol con-
tradict the NHTSA employee's claim. Alcohol or other drugs have
been implicated in not only 50-70% of drownings, boating and
snowmobile accidents, but also workplace incidents, where work-
ers are "supposed" to be sober. There is no reason to believe that
the percentage of on-the-road accidents attributable to alcohol
would be much lower.

My innate skepticism about bureaucracy and government in
general suggests that if the public knew the likelihood of alcohol
being involved in any accident, they might insist that all participants be tested. This could fill the courts with DUIs.

The first line of offense in the battle to get addicts sober is to
have as many of them as possible arrested for DUI. When more are
apprehended early in their disease, fewer will inflict harm on or
destroy their families, careers and the lives of others with whom

they come in contact. Instead of filling prisons with hard-core criminals and allowing people to suffer the private effects of alcoholism by way of fatherless children, broken homes, ended marriages and lost jobs, we can temporarily fill them with DUIs. To suggest that we have this opportunity when a minimum of 499 out of 500 incidents of drinking and driving do not result in arrest is to point out the obvious. Blood-tested sobriety as a condition of early release and parole just might one day result in nearly empty prisons. Countless addicts have chosen sobriety over incarceration when offered this alternative.

One recovering alcoholic was quoted in the "Big Book" of Alcoholics Anonymous as saying, "I wish everyone could be in A.A., and if everyone were there would be no need for jails, in my opinion."[1] Initially, sobriety usually requires attendance at A.A. meetings. His point is, if every addict were clean and sober, there would be no crime. This may not be much of an exaggeration, considering the fact that there were no arrests at the 2000 Alcoholics Anonymous International Convention in Minneapolis, Minnesota, with 90,000 in attendance. The Chief of Police commented that this was the first time ever that this occurred with a group so large. Remember: active addiction causes destructive behaviors, not the other way around.

3. Inability to multi-task.

Police officers, when pulling someone over, usually ask for a license and vehicle registration simultaneously. The reason for this is that a driver with a high BAL may forget a document, produce a different one or fumble with his wallet or papers. While he searches for the requested items, the officer may also ask a distracting question such as, "Where are you going?" or, "Can you tell me what time it is without looking at your watch?" This is known as "dividing attention." If there's a lot of alcohol in the suspect's system, he may stop what he's doing, respond to the question and then produce the wrong documents. This works because the inebriated person cannot easily do two things at once.

Again, this is not the case for the highly tolerant alcoholic. Officers catch the more obvious drunks, but often not those in early-stage addiction who don't show the "obvious" signs of inebriation at BALs that would have the rest of us on our faces. For example, they probably wouldn't have arrested Elizabeth Taylor had they pulled her over, even if she had been drinking heavily. In the early 1980s, she checked into the Betty Ford Clinic seeking help for her dependence on prescription drugs. After two weeks, she realized that she had a problem with alcohol as well, which is true for all addicts who use this drug. (By her own testimony, Taylor could drink ex-husband Richard Burton, himself an alcoholic of stature, under the table.) The amazing thing was, according to her she had never been "drunk," meaning she never displayed obvious signs of inebriation. Due to this incredibly high tolerance to alcohol, few law enforcers would have suspected a BAL in excess of the legal limit.

Non-addicts who rarely drink can have a BAL as low as .04 per cent (two drinks in quick succession for a 200-pound person or just one for a 100-pounder) and appear inebriated. Addicts can achieve BALs as high as .24 per cent (12 drinks in quick succession for the 200-pounder) before slurring words, staggering or showing other signs of intoxication. This is the reason we need to look at behaviors to determine the probability of addiction. We may never see an alcoholic "drunk," but the behaviors will, at some point, turn destructive, whether this occurs behind the wheel of a car or privately, behind closed doors.

4. One set of tires on a line (45%).

This may be related to the inability to multi-task at high BALs. The DUI, concentrating on driving in a straight line so that he doesn't look like an obvious drunk, keeps a set of wheels on the white or yellow lane boundary. Don't ask him to stop quickly if traffic comes to a standstill. Just get out of the way of anyone driving like this and, if there are any other signs, report him.

5. Straddling line, with the center or lane marker in-between the wheels (65%).

The same comments can be made as for a driver with one set of tires on a line. Except this one, if he's drunk, is *really* drunk. Get out of his way and do what you can to keep others clear. I've seen someone this wasted only once. Good thing he was on a wide-open freeway. He confirmed DUI by intermittently weaving, braking for no apparent reason and slowing to 30 mph. I turned on my emergency flashers and began weaving between two lanes of traffic, making others aware of a serious problem up ahead. Unfortunately, mobile phone use wasn't yet common. It was also long before I understood alcoholism and the importance of helping addicts get arrested, so I exited at my intended turnoff.

6. Driving on a shoulder (55%).

Over the years, we've all seen many vehicles driving on the shoulder. We probably assumed the driver was looking for something that may have blown out of the window or he was having car trouble. While this may be true in some cases, according to the NHTSA study there's a 55% probability that such a person is simply intoxicated. It's interesting that this clue, which some may not even imagine is suggestive of DUI, is in fact such a good indicator.

7. Abruptly swerving (55%).

The NHTSA study found that 45% of abrupt swerves resulted from driver error or good reason, such as an animal or other obstacle on the road. However, the cause was shown to be inebriation more than half the time.

I recently saw someone abruptly swerve twice for no reason as he approached a freeway exit. I intended to report him, but he zipped through a stop sign at about 20 mph at the bottom of the off-ramp and sped away at near freeway speeds in a residential neighborhood. Too bad he wasn't apprehended: he was wielding a dangerous weapon in the form of 2,500 pounds of metal, plastic and rubber—possibly in your neighborhood.

8. Drifting (50%).

While this could be from falling asleep at the wheel (which can be just as dangerous as DUI) or other factors, half the time it's a sign of being under the influence. In any case, get out of the way! He may ram you from behind or from the side.

9. Riding the brakes (45%).

I've driven with non-drinkers who tend to do this, which may account for the fact that this was found to be a sign of intoxication in only 45% of such incidences. However, if someone is observed alternating between riding the brakes and accelerating, tailgating the vehicle ahead and falling back, then repeating the cycle, you have multiple clues to insobriety.

Recall that the (conservative) computation in the DRE manual suggests that we take the higher probability observation and add 10% for each additional clue. This usually results in a greater-than-50% chance that a DUI is in progress with only two tested and validated clues evident, by itself a perfectly good reason to dial 911.

10. Unnecessary braking (45%).

Slightly over half the time, a driver brakes unnecessarily because he thinks he has missed his exit, believes something is on the road, or has another reason that turns out to be an error of sober perception. Yet, 45% of the time when we observe this behavior, the driver is DUI. And we thought that there were just a bunch of poor drivers on the road!

11. Backing into traffic (45%).

Once again, this may be caused by simple driver error. Sometimes there's a blind spot, or someone crawls into traffic carefully and just doesn't see a fast-approaching vehicle. Usually, a sober driver will do everything he can to see if anyone is near, including maneuvering so that he can get a better view of oncoming traffic.

However, forty-five per cent of the time, the driver backing up is DUI. If you hit him, be sure to ask that an officer administer the standardized field sobriety test. Also, watch the suspect's every move while waiting for the officer to arrive. You don't want to be asked in the courtroom whether you can be certain he didn't drink after the incident, causing the BAL to increase to a level in excess of the legal limit. As a non-addict or clean and sober addict, you are no match for the practicing one in ability to tell extremely convincing un-truths.

Can't imagine that an addict would make such a claim? Just remember the fellow who denied that he was the culprit evading the tollbooth 705 times. Recovering addicts aren't kidding when they tell us they were the world's greatest liars. They have been known to beat a DUI on this very argument, with the stress of the accident "causing" them to drink "immediately after."

12. Slow response to traffic signal (40%).
When the signal turns green, he just sits there. You wonder if he'll ever move. He's either sloppy drunk or not paying attention. Another clue will help to confirm. As with all of these, if there are no secondary clues after a period of time, we should consider the possibility that there was simply a human at the wheel, prone to making occasional errors. It is addicts who repeat destructive behaviors, including driving mistakes they wouldn't make in long-term sobriety.

13. Accelerating or decelerating much more rapidly than traffic conditions require (30%)
Rapid acceleration squanders fuel, while such deceleration unnecessarily wears the brakes. Normally, sober people don't fritter away things they work hard for. Addicts may do this to show off, or they may be so drunk that the pedals are difficult to touch without a jerkiness of action that results in sudden movements. Although the NHTSA study found that this is at the lower end of DUI probabilities, we want to be aware of all reasonably valid clues. Even a likelihood of 30% is very useful. After all, this increases the odds of possible addiction by three-fold in someone we don't even know, as well as the probability that a randomly selected driver is DUI by as much as a factor of fifteen (30% vs. 2% of all drivers DUI during weekday daylight hours).

14. Positioning to accelerate and decelerate rapidly (30%).
Sober drivers plan ahead. Even if the speeding up and slowing down is not "more rapidly than conditions require," most drivers don't put themselves into a position of repeatedly having to do so. This behavior, which the NHTSA study reports is a result of DUI about 30% of the time, is probably a matter of poor judgment.

15. Stopping abruptly (30%), not at an intersection (as in stop and go traffic).

Have you ever come close to hitting someone from behind because he stopped abruptly? Maybe he wasn't just a "bad" driver, or even a good one making a mistake. He may have been someone who was DUI. Tired of having to slam on my brakes and risk being hit from behind, I once switched lanes just in time. This is an instance where the probability of DUI when multiple clues are observed may be significantly lowballed by the method suggested in the DRE Manual. Recall that it suggests adding 10% for each additional clue. This should include observing the same behavior twice (for those clues that don't require repeated observations). With proper testing, it might be found that if a driver were to stop in a particularly abrupt manner more than once in a short period of time, the probability of DUI is double or even triple the original 30%.

16. Stopping too abruptly (30%) at an intersection.

This is a variation of "rapid deceleration." The NHTSA study didn't distinguish these from vehicles not at an intersection. My hunch is that this isn't as good a clue when the abrupt stop is made at an intersection, since at least there's an apparent reason to stop. If this is the only sign of DUI, even when repeated the driver may simply lack good driving skills. However if other clues are observed, pay heed.

17. Poor merging.

A driver who doesn't properly merge with the traffic flow, especially at freeway on ramps, is clearly endangering others. It is surprising that the NHTSA study didn't mention this behavior, but there may have been too few observations or perhaps a lack of clear definition as to what constitutes "poor." We can probably safely assume that the less competent the merging, the greater the likelihood of DUI.

Poor merging is usually a case of entering a freeway too slowly, given the flow of traffic. We should be alert to the possibility of DUI and be cognizant of other clues. One that may follow is driving at more than 10 mph under the speed limit, which we will later identify as a sign of probable DUI.

18. Turning with a wide radius (65%) ("squaring the turn").

The NHTSA study found this to be one of the two most likely indicators of DUI. This is interesting, since many other indications could be considered more suspicious. Apparently, the visual perception of a person under the influence is so distorted that this behavior becomes far more common among drunks than those sober. Keep in mind that the probabilities take into account the relatively small number of DUIs versus the far larger proportion of non-DUIs. Consider this example: if 2% of drivers are DUI with these accounting for 65% of all turns with a wide radius, we might conclude that non-DUIs rarely make these maneuvers. However, while the DUI is about 80 times more likely to do this than the non-DUI [(65/2) / (35/98) = 80], the absolute number of times may be high for everyone. It is the relative number of occasions that these odds measure, not the absolute number.

19. Running a red light, but not speeding up to do so.

The reason drunks sometimes sit at traffic signals for several seconds after the light has turned green is not just because their reaction times are slowed. The law of inertia seems to apply to those with enough alcohol in their systems. A body at rest will remain that way, while one in motion tends to continue moving at the same speed and direction.

The drunk may "see" the green light for several seconds after it has turned yellow or red. This misperception results in running the signal. One possible reason the NHTSA study didn't connect this with DUI is because an inordinately large number of addicts who run reds may be sober drunks or those with less blood alcohol, speeding up in an attempt to make the yellow light. These drivers are often those who fall under the categories "I am invincible" and "Supreme Being complex," not considering the potentially lethal consequences of their actions.

20. Making a left turn in front of someone with inadequate distance.

Depth and distance perception is affected at BALs generally as low as .04 to .06 per cent, becoming more distorted as the alcohol level increases. The possibility that many of these left turns fall into the "I am invincible" category (clue #7) may be the reason the NHTSA found relatively few under the influence at the time of the violation. However, if the study differentiated between those who speed up versus those who appear more lackadaisical, a high percentage of the latter might be found to be legally intoxicated.

21. Failing to yield the right of way, but without an attitude.
Poor judgment may be a sign that a driver is having a bad day or thoughts are elsewhere. Or, he just may be high as a kite. Since not yielding may suggest he's heading in a direction different from yours, you generally won't have the opportunity to follow up and find more clues. However, if a police officer sees this, he should check for sobriety to make sure that the behavior can be properly chalked up to simple driver error.

22. Unusually slow in pulling over for an emergency vehicle.
Since hearing loss and decreased peripheral vision occur at high blood alcohol levels, an emergency vehicle may not be heard or seen by a DUI. This driver may also have the stereo turned up, further impairing his awareness of the world around him. Of course, the self-centered practicing addict, usually a fine human being in sobriety, couldn't care less.

23. Passing on a two-lane highway with inadequate distance.
This sign of impaired judgment may be the result of DUI. However, it could simply be (very dangerous) driver error or just lack of experience. A few years ago I arranged to have someone pulled over for behavior that to me suggested DUI. On a wide open two-lane desert highway, a young driver attempted to pass me at 72 mph while I was going 70 mph. This wouldn't have been so dangerous except for the fact that a big semi was rapidly approaching. I quickly slowed to 50 mph, allowing him to pass safely. A half-hour later, an officer was able to ticket the 17-year-old driver for doing 75 mph in a 65-mph zone. He detected no alcohol. I was given the option of making a private person's arrest, but was told that the kid would likely lose his license anyway, already having had a couple of tickets on his record over the last six months. Not yet fully understanding the importance of proactively assisting people to experience all the consequences for their misbehaviors and wishing to avoid having to appear as a witness 200 miles from home, I opted to let the officer cite him.

Although the serious error in judgment was probably due to inexperience, if this occurred today I would ask that the standardized field sobriety test be administered, especially to determine if there might be a combination of low levels of alcohol and sedatives. These two drugs could conceivably cause the style of passing that I observed, which potentially endangered both our lives.

The effect of a combination of drugs, called "potentiation," even though well-known and used to its fullest by most addicts, is poorly understood by virtually all non-addicts. The mixing of two drugs does not just double the effect. It makes the effects of both far more powerful and potentially lethal. Combine for example, a couple of shots of alcohol with a similarly small dose of sedatives, barbiturates, amphetamines or other drug, and the person taking these will be stoned.

This mixing is common among those who wish to hide their use or its extent. In this way, officers, spouses, co-workers and employers are far less likely to detect an odor. Since smelling like, or being observed guzzling, whiskey or vodka isn't "ladylike," many addict housewives and female bar patrons will mix various drugs. The Betty Ford Clinic estimates that well over two-thirds of female alcoholics are such poly-drug addicts. They often won't even test over the legal blood alcohol level. A .05 per cent BAL with a small amount of some other drug will not set off any alarms, even though it causes the alcoholic to act in destructive ways.

This is the reason so many addicts over-dose. A false sense of invincibility can lead addicts to combine in fatal ways as they try to reach a high that only they can experience. John Belushi is a perfect example of this. He combined heroin and cocaine, otherwise known as a "speedball." He overdosed...and died.

24. Weaving (60%).

This is the classic sign, in which over-steering in one direction is compensated for by over-steering in the other. It is a clue to a sloppy drunk, usually one at a very high BAL. As is the case for all clues in this section, he's dangerous more because of a slowed reaction time than for being overly aggressive or reckless in his actions.

We all know that we should get out of the way of drunks in the "poor judgment" section. One could ask what percent of the fatalities in which alcohol is a factor result from these versus the clues in the first two categories ("I am invincible" and "Supreme Being complex"). There is anecdotal evidence (real life stories without double-blind studies) that a large number of fatal accidents can be attributed to driving behaviors of the earlier-stage, more functional alcoholic who can usually be identified by the actions described in the earlier categories. Now we know that we should get out of the way, regardless.

1. *Alcoholics Anonymous: The Story of How Many Thousands of Men and Women Have Recovered From Alcoholism,* New York: Alcoholics Anonymous World Services, Inc., Third Edition, 1976, p. 542.

5

Apparent Mental Confusion

This category, like "poor judgment," may also be filled with more obvious drunks. It could account for the fact that these clues were more frequently found to be statistically significant of actual DUI in the NHTSA study than those in the first two categories ("Sense of Invincibility" and "Supreme Being").

The following clues can be attributed to confusion due to unfamiliarity with the area. On the other hand, they may be signs of heavy sedation brought on by excessive drinking/drug use. These addicts are not likely in-between drinks, having passed through the "Supreme Being complex" and "I am invincible" stages of either that day's imbibing specifically or addiction generally. Often, they are continuously stoned.

1. Erratic gestures.

Those under the influence can be especially animated in their "hand signals." They may be talking to a passenger, real or imaginary or gesturing wildly to someone outside their vehicle. The more erratic and longer in duration, the greater the likelihood that something is seriously amiss. If combined with one other clue, I would assume DUI, for my own safety as well as yours.

2. Driving in turn-only lane, straight, without turning (55%).

There's either some serious confusion here, or someone who's really drunk and greatly endangering the lives of others. Many sober drivers have entered the turn-only lane and realize they have erred. These drivers either make the turn anyway or stop and re-enter the flow of traffic when safe to do so. However, the person described in this clue keeps on truckin'. Calling 911 emergency should be considered if any other secondary clues to DUI are observed.

3. Driving slower than 10 mph below the speed limit (50%).

Neither the NHTSA study nor I mention driving 10 mph over the limit as a clue to DUI (except with children in tow or weaving through traffic). Driving extra slowly, however, is a good sign of being very, very drunk (or very, very old). Fortunately, if there's an accident, at least it is less likely to be damaging than one involving a fast-driving, high-functioning, early-stage addict.

4. Stopping without cause in a traffic lane (50%).

Here's another clue in which the driver is either very confused or very stoned. It's also one in which if there were any other signs present, I wouldn't hesitate to report a likely DUI. An instance in which I observed such erratic driving was one of those real-life experiences that inspired me to obtain a mobile phone. An obviously intoxicated man repeatedly drove a few hundred yards, stopped and made U-turns. More curious than anything else, I watched him move slower than the flow of traffic while not impeding, stopping only after traffic passed. If there had been an accident, he probably wouldn't have killed anyone at these speeds. Of course, as erratic as drunks can be, it shouldn't be a surprise if he suddenly flew off at 90 mph. Now, with my mobile phone, I'd hang out until the cops arrive.

5. Erratic braking (45%).

This may be related to the poor judgment responsible for unnecessary braking or the riding of brakes (discussed in "Poor Judgment," numbers 9 and 10). However, the word "erratic" suggests confusion and not simply impaired judgment. If it were not for drivers' confusion while looking for intended destinations in unfamiliar areas, this clue might provide a far higher probability of DUI. On the other hand, since only 10% of drivers are alcoholics, and at most times of day only 2% of all persons on the road are DUI, a finding that drivers exhibiting this single clue are DUI 45% of the time is very useful information.

6. Driving the wrong way on a one-way street (45%).

Living in an area without one-way streets, it has always been easy for me (being somewhat absent-minded anyway) to begin driving in the wrong direction, especially when there is no traffic moving on that street. If you were to observe this, you would want to look for other signs of intoxication and, in the meantime, assume that he was DUI. Any cop who sees this should pull the driver over and test for sobriety. Anyone else should call 911 emergency if other signs are observed.

Every so often, driving behaviors are exhibited by each of us that could arouse suspicion—after all, we're only human. We just don't slip all the time, repeatedly and with numerous other indications of DUI or addiction.

7. Signaling inconsistent with one's actions (40%).

As is the case for many in this section, if the driver is DUI, he probably has a very high BAL. It's possible that the reason the likelihood of being under the influence is only 40% is that this takes into account those signaling right or left and heading straight. It also takes into consideration those signaling one way and moving or turning in the opposite direction. The former may simply not realize the turn signal is on, since the noise feature could be broken or radio and/or road noise could be drowning it out. The latter driver, turning opposite the signaled intention, is probably quite drunk. This is an obvious sign of DUI that many learn in driver education class.

8. Stopping far short of an intersection (subcategory of stopping inappropriately--35%).

The 65% who are not DUI but do this are probably those looking for something, such as a street address, which often proves annoyingly elusive in commercial areas due to poor signage. I may have appeared to be DUI on a number of occasions while looking for such an address because I was driving too slowly and even stopped short of an intersection, wondering which lane was the proper one. If addresses were more visible, this clue would probably be a better one, since eliminating this problem would reduce the number of "false positives" (in which the clue falsely suggests the possibility of DUI).

9. Stopping inappropriately at a crosswalk (subcategory of stopping inappropriately--35%).

It's much safer to stop your car than to keep moving if you think that someone may be crossing. This type of concern or looking for a street name may be the non-DUI cause of this behavior.

However, 35% of the time there is no reasonable cause—the driver is merely drunk. So, about two-thirds of the time we should feel empathy—after all, we've all been lost—but a third of the time we should hope he avoids killing a pedestrian he doesn't see.

10. Stopping for a green light, or for a flashing yellow (subcategory of stopping inappropriately--35%).

If drunk, this driver may be more disoriented (read: has an even more elevated BAL) than the person who continues to wait after the signal turns green. However, stopping for a flashing yellow could simply be a sign of legitimate confusion. After all, such signals are rarely seen in many areas and can confound out-of-towners.

11. Illegal or abrupt turn (35%).

This is a generic catchall that the following three clues do not specifically address, including making a right turn on red where prohibited and a left turn during times of day when not permitted.

12. Turning sharply from a wrong lane (35%).

This is a driver who, even though not in the right or left-turn lane, proceeds to turn sharply and often quickly. The sober person, realizing he's about to miss his turnoff, usually decides to continue on. The addict, tolerating frustration poorly, has a greater tendency to decide at the last moment to turn from the wrong lane. Hopefully, he doesn't turn into you. It should be mentioned that the inebriated person might not have planned his route, which tends to cause this sort of situation to occur more frequently.

13. Illegal U-turn (35%).

This is a clue that one might think can't possibly be valid; after all, most of us at some point make illegal U-turns. However, this is a good example in which repeated violations become important to the calculation of odds. If the question were, "Have you ever made a U-turn illegally?" this clue would be worthless. Instead, we ascribe a probability to each U-turn. This makes use of the fact that alcoholics (DUI or not) repeat this behavior far more frequently than do non-alcoholics.

Take out your calculators for just a moment. If 5% of drivers commit 35% of these infractions while 95% commit 65%, we can determine that DUIs make illegal U-turns about ten times more frequently than non-DUIs. This assumes that 5% of those driving at night (when the NHTSA study was conducted) were intoxicated. (The math is: 95/5 = 19. 19 x 35 = 665. 665/65 = approximately 10.)

The same idea is true for virtually all these clues. Each of us display many of the behaviors from time to time, which makes the question, "Have you ever…" useless. The fact that addicts engage in these behaviors far more often than do non-addicts is what makes all of these clues helpful.

14. Turning from outside a designated turn lane (35%).

This is the more gentle, rounded turn from the wrong lane. The DUI that executes this kind of turn is probably a bit more inebriated than the drunk driver who turns "sharply." He is, therefore, more likely to display other signs of confusion. Look for these if offered the opportunity!

15. Headlights not on when required (30%).

The NHTSA study doesn't include observations of "daylight headlight test" zones that we see on dangerous two-lane rural highways, where a head-on collision will usually cost both parties their lives. However, high blood alcohol levels, which make multitasking difficult, may cause the DUI to forget to turn his lights on when required, even at night. I have noticed that reckless drivers often fail to follow "daylight test" zone rules, while those with headlights on are rarely seen driving recklessly. It is likely that the greater the need for headlights, the higher the probability of DUI with the lights out. One DRE officer told me that he's noticed that if it's "really" dark, there's about a 70% probability of DUI for a person driving with headlights off.

16. Erratic movements inside the vehicle.

My wife and I once watched a driver repeatedly lean over to the passenger side of his van. This was occurring in the fast lane of a freeway with stop-and-go traffic moving at an average speed of about 20 mph. This was an excellent clue to the amazing event that we were about to witness. He swerved onto the inside (fast lane) shoulder twice before approaching a concrete median construction barrier sitting about one foot from the fast lane. I said to my wife, "I think he's going to hit the barrier," which in my opinion was too close even for sober drivers. Leaving plenty of room in case his vehicle careened out of control, we watched him sideswipe the barrier not once, but several times. Despite three separate calls to 911, he was not apprehended. This is one of several unfortunate incidents that inspire a number of the public policy recommendations made later.

Note that the erratic movements inside the vehicle put us on notice that the driver might be DUI. This supports the general rule that any degree of bizarre or destructive behavior inside or outside the vehicle could alert us to the possibility that we may be observing an addict. We should always act accordingly, until and unless proven otherwise.

6

Physical Signs of Person or Vehicle

"You can't tell a book by its cover" is an old, overused and misunderstood cliché. When it comes to people, oftentimes the "cover" can be used to form hypotheses that may keep us out of harm's way. For example, sun, smoking and booze can take their toll on the face. In my capacity as an Enrolled Agent, preparing tax returns and engaging in tax planning, I once told a 47-year-old that withdrawing funds from a pension would result in a certain amount of tax, completely overlooking the premature withdrawal penalty for those under age 59 1/2. The reason for this is because he looked well over 65. (I also jumped to this conclusion about his age due to the fact that he was retiring after 30 years of service with a public utility. I have made very few errors in my professional career, but this one was a doozy.) When I prepared his return the following year, I realized that the penalty applied, resulting in a very unfortunate and costly situation. Today, the mere fact of having a need or desire to withdraw from retirement savings early alerts me to the possibility that something may be amiss. His heavily wrinkled face was, of course, at least partially a result of 30+ years of active alcohol and other drug addiction.

This is just one example of the numerous physical clues, which by themselves are not definitive, but can cue us in to the possibility of addiction and DUI.

1. Smoking.

The likelihood that someone smoking in the United States is an alcoholic is about 33%. The math is simple. About 90% of alcoholics in the U.S. are believed to be smokers. We also have a pretty clear idea that about 10% of the country's adult population are alcoholics.[1] Therefore, 9%, 90% of 10%, are both alcoholics and smokers.

The most recent statistics disclose that almost 27% of Americans over the age of 18 smoke. Since 9% of this 27% are smokers who are also alcohol and other drug addicts, we can deduce that about 9/27, or 33% of smokers, are alcoholics. Note that the smaller the denominator (the bottom number in the fraction), the greater the usefulness of this indicator in determining a likelihood of alcoholism. In Japan and China, where practically everyone smokes and the denominator is as high as 80% among adult males, this is not a useful clue. On the other hand, in California, where less than 20% of the population smokes, the odds that a smoker is also an alcoholic may be as high as 45% (9/20).

Thank God alcoholics are not always drinking while smoking. However, it is a helpful clue in identifying possible alcoholism. As we have shown, the behaviors of the addict in-between drinking episodes can be every bit as erratic and dangerous as those of a DUI in progress. It is an excellent clue to DUI as well, if any of the behaviors from categories three and four ("poor judgment," "mental confusion") are observed.

2. Chewing gum combined with any reckless behavior, poor judgment or evidence of mental confusion.

Ok, I can hear the gnashing of teeth on this one (even from those of you not chewing). Remember, I've been known to drive in the wrong direction down a one-way street. Just because you chew gum doesn't mean you're a drunk. However, gum, breath mints, mouthwash and heavy perfume or cologne are valid clues to the possibility that the person observed (driving or not) is hiding the stench of alcohol or another drug. Desperate prison inmates and other surreptitious users often drink mouthwash just for the alcohol (remember the story of Kitty Dukakis, wife of 1988 Presidential contender Michael Dukakis, drinking mouthwash and rubbing alcohol when no other liquor was available).

A client in my professional practice as an Enrolled Agent had repeated financial difficulties. I wasn't thinking of addiction, but one day realized that I had failed to consider an important clue: he'd been very ill with heart and other health issues for years. Yes, serious illness can cause financial problems. However, there are also 350 secondary diseases and disorders, including cancer and heart disease, which include alcoholism as a contributing factor.[2] Therefore, serious or repeated illness can clue us in to possible addiction. I was discussing poor health and its link to addiction with a friend of his, who was intimately aware of both the financial situation and the health of my client. He responded as if a light bulb went off in his head: "Have you ever noticed how much cologne he wears? He hides the smell of booze from heavy drinking!" I was then told of numerous other clues to which I hadn't previously been made aware, including instances of spousal abuse and being verbally abusive to friends. We agreed on a diagnosis of alcoholism.

This underscores the usefulness of sharing information with close others. There needs to be a wide understanding of the problem and its extent to encourage enough friends, family, coworkers and others to become involved in an intervention. Subtle clues are all that most observers will ever find. It is only when we piece together these seemingly unimportant, isolated clues that we can begin to see addiction. If we don't suspect it, we will never confirm it. If we don't confirm it, we will never intervene. If we don't intervene, tragedy will occur, eventually.

The importance of raising the antennae when even one apparently minor clue is found, cannot be emphasized strongly enough. One such clue is the simple act of drinking. About 70% of U.S. adults use the drug alcohol. Since 10% of the U.S. population consists of alcoholics, one out of seven, or almost 15% of drinkers have alcoholism. This seemingly minor increase in the odds isn't so small when we think of it as a 50% increase (from 10% to 15%). There are no known statistics on gum chewing or some of the other clues that will be suggested in this section. While the odds of DUI or alcoholism are probably considerably less than 30% for each of these clues, they are likely equal to or greater than 15%. To emphasize the importance of connecting these with other clues so that we do not begin seeing an addict behind every steering wheel, we will repeat "combined with" any reckless behavior, etc. for such "minor" clues. However, bear in mind how small the number "seven" is. Observe three couples and one single friend who drink. The odds are 50-50 that one is an alcoholic.

3. Window wide open on a hot or cold day combined with any reckless behavior, poor judgment or evidence of mental confusion.

Granted, there are a number of reasons why someone might drive with their windows open. However, it doesn't diminish the importance of the following story. One day, I saw a fairly new Ford Taurus with California plates speeding through traffic and tailgating on a hot summer day in Southern California. His windows were wide open. Now, chances are, that late model car came with air-conditioning. Why wasn't he using it? It suddenly dawned on me that I had seen a number of people driving recklessly with their windows down. A Drug Recognition Expert explained this common phenomenon. The addict who does this is, like one chewing gum, hiding the odor or in this case dispersing it outside his vehicle. He figures that if pulled over, he is less likely to be arrested. Recall that alcoholism is a biological process and, therefore, has nothing to do with intelligence. Many addicts, just like non-addicts, can be brilliant and clever. It's unfortunate that they so often use their mental energy drumming up ways to hide their drug or the extent of its use, rather than channeling their creativity into more productive pursuits.

4. Drinking anything combined with any reckless behavior, poor judgment or evidence of mental confusion.

That may or may not be water in the Perrier bottle. Alcoholics, as mentioned, often hide their liquor. One way is to add booze to a bottle of water, can of soda or cup of coffee. These are containers that few would ever suspect. Yet, even when mixed with the container's original non-alcoholic beverage, they can hold enough alcohol to maintain a high BAL. Remember, the alcoholic often "pre-drinks" and needs only the equivalent of six to nine ounces of beer or about an ounce of 80-proof liquor per hour to maintain an already elevated BAL. The average non-alcoholic would never suspect that someone appearing to be health conscious by drinking pure water, or even coffee for the reason of staying alert, might be an addict. For example, I wasn't the least bit suspicious while my ex-fiancée drank Lipton iced teas spiked with vodka in the original Lipton bottle. To insure that I would not ask questions, she hid the residual odor with gum and mouthwash. I just figured that she always wanted to be ready for a kiss!

Many more methods of hiding liquor and other drugs are discussed in my book, *Drunks, Drugs & Debits*. A few that warrant mention include beer in Martinelli's bottles and substituting Bailey's Irish Cream for regular coffee cream in that commuter mug or Starbucks cup. One story that comes to mind has to do with four college students on a road trip. Before they left, they stocked up on Coca-Cola in an ice chest. They also cleaned out their windshield washer container in their car and replaced the fluid with rum. Running the washer fluid leads under the dash into the car allowed them to have rum and Coke on tap by merely activating the windshield wiper fluid mechanism. Just in case you think this is a great idea, this story was first told by one of those college students while attending a DUI class. There are even stories of small town cops with such links in the dashboards of their police cars.

Alcoholics will go to extraordinary lengths to protect their perceived right to drink anywhere and under any conditions. We have no idea what's in that bottle, glass, can or mug. If there are any behavioral signs of intoxication (i.e., destructive or bizarre behaviors), it's best not to assume truth in packaging.

5. Head out the window (60%).

A dog's ears flapping in the wind is cute. A drunk's ears are not. If a person has his head outside the window, a sign for which the NHTSA found a 60% probability of DUI, we should immediately begin looking for behaviors that may be dangerous to others. Other than neighbors calling out to friends or drivers asking directions, there doesn't seem to be a valid reason for holding one's head out the window. Blow drying one's hair, or trying to remain awake, are not valid reasons.

6. Tightly gripping the wheel (60%).

Who'd ever dream that white knuckling it in an 11 o'clock-1 o'clock position would signal such a high probability of DUI? Apparently, this has to do with the addict's inability to multi-task at high BALs, as he attempts to focus purely on what lies ahead. He may not see something coming from behind or either side, and he might not react quickly enough to avoid an obstacle in front, but at least he will see it as he crashes. On the other hand, that doesn't mean he'll remember it.

7. Slouching in seat (60%).

The NHTSA study found that this form of poor posture is a good clue to DUI. At very high BALs, muscle tone diminishes and relaxation sets in. The fact that alcoholics are better able to roll with the punches may account for a higher crash survival rate than among the victims, although recent studies indicate this may be a myth.

8. Face close to windshield (60%).

This may be a sign of a very high BAL due to the need to concentrate. The suspect is willing to experience some discomfort in order to focus mightily on what he's doing.

9. Eye fixation (60%).

Again, the addict is doing what he can to concentrate on what lies ahead, missing much of anything else that may be occurring around him. Part of defensive driving involves keeping your eyes moving, which includes checking mirrors, side streets, etc. The DUI with a high BAL tends to stare straight ahead.

10. Covering one eye with the hand or closing one eye.

DREs tell me they have actually arrested DUIs on the basis of this one clue. I have been told by recovering addicts that they have done this (one for two hundred miles) and not gotten caught. Obviously, the driver is so blasted he's seeing double. There's not much that one can say regarding some of these clues other than "wow."

11. Any other physical clue that suggests the driver appears to be drunk (60%).

Partying or engaging in a visibly heated argument inside a vehicle are two such clues. I once saw four 20-year-olds in a car having a good ol' time. Pulling up beside them at a stoplight, I saw four pairs of very glassy eyes inside their vehicle. "Glassy eyes" was the only telltale sign of Henri Paul being drunk in the hotel video prior to the Princess Diana tragedy. This fact should be considered by anyone proclaiming, "But it's not my business."

12. Extremely loud music combined with any reckless behavior, poor judgment or evidence of mental confusion.

I'd occasionally be busted on this one in terms of just loud music. In addition, due to an apparent endorphin rush I get from listening to my favorite tunes turned way up, I have to be careful about speeding. It took three tickets in as many years to realize what was happening. I experimented with the music at different levels and, when I didn't pay attention to the speedometer, I found myself driving about five to eight miles per hour faster when the music was blasting. I also realized that for some 25 years almost all my cars were stick shifts, during which time I had only a few tickets. I now often drive in 2nd gear (in an automatic, no less) on city streets, causing the engine to brake, making it far more difficult to drive over the speed limit. While always alert to the possibility of DUI after observing only one identifying behavior, this is another example of the reason we generally need two or more clues before ascribing a high enough probability to consider notifying authorities.

However, loud noise of any kind may be an excellent clue late at night in residential neighborhoods. Turning up the volume on the stereo to ridiculous levels or revving up an engine with loud exhaust pipes shows a lack of consideration for others that is best explained by addiction.

13. Flashy or very large vehicle combined with any reckless behavior, poor judgment or evidence of mental confusion.

The addict must inflate his ego, which often takes form in the belief that "I am better than you and I have and deserve the best of everything regardless of cost or ability to pay." A flashy vehicle could easily be in the "Supreme Being complex" category, but is listed here because it is solid physical evidence. Please don't misconstrue: there are plenty of people driving such vehicles who are not addicts, just as virtually every non-addict occasionally engages in suspect behaviors. However, when combined with other signs, the odds of DUI and, therefore, alcoholism increase substantially.

One owner said he drives a large truck because, "It's the hormones. We want to be bigger than the other guy on the road." Another said, "Guys look at you like you've got some testosterone. The No. 1 reason I bought this truck? I like the way I look in it."[3] These are clearly ego-based attitudes, central to alcoholism.

14. Looks like a "druggie" type.

If he walks and talks like one, he probably is. This wouldn't have worked in the 1970s, when so many non-addicts used drugs along with their addict friends (with the exception of those recently running for President or other office), and looked the part. However, it probably works in the early 2000s, especially for anyone past adolescence.

15. Vehicle with lots of nicks and dents combined with any reckless behavior, poor judgment or evidence of mental confusion.

This is another clue for which I could be convicted if we look only at the car. Due to a genetic eye disorder, I don't have binocular vision. As a result, I've nicked my vehicle more than once, usually when entering tricky parking spaces. Also, as a skier I have found that other skiers tend to be rather careless in carrying gear from their cars to the slopes. Why bother fixing such nicks and dents when I'm just going to go through the same process again next year?

However, if I saw my car and there were other signs of DUI, I'd suspect me. Keep in mind, our thinking does not originate in or need confirmation from a court of law. We need to identify possible DUIs, to protect both others and ourselves.

16. Vehicle obviously not taken care of combined with any reckless behavior, poor judgment or evidence of mental confusion.

This could be a dirty vehicle, inside and/or out. A brilliant physicist, less concerned with looks than substance, may have a car in this condition. On the other hand, its owner may be a latter-stage addict who doesn't and can't afford to care, due to time spent and money squandered on alcohol and/or other drugs.

17. SUV combined with any reckless behavior, poor judgment or evidence of mental confusion.

This could almost be listed as simply, "Sports Utility Vehicle" and placed in the "Supreme Being complex" category. However, even though a convincing argument will be made that SUV owners are more likely addicts than the 10% in the overall U.S. population, the likelihood is probably not even as high as 30%, the level of significance one might hope to reach in stand-alone clues. It was also deemed best to save potentially the most controversial clue, a physical indication, for last. Like all the others, by itself this clue is not definitive. There are plenty of reasons to own an SUV having nothing to do with inflating one's ego. These include safety for self and family, space for transporting tools and goods, hauling boats and trailers, ease of operation in snow and the much-vaunted off-road capabilities. However, surveys have found that many SUV owners are not interested in these features. Only 15% of SUVs have ever—even once—been driven off-road, despite this being the most distinguishing physical and advertised feature separating these vehicles from vans and station wagons.

There is, instead, a gaping psychological difference between owners of SUVs and minivans.⁴ According to research conducted by both DaimlerChrysler and General Motors, both SUV and minivan buyers want to be "in control." However, this has a very different meaning to these two groups. Minivan owners want to be in control in terms of safety and maneuverability in parking and traffic. According to Fred J. Schaafsma, a top GM vehicle development engineer, many SUV owners want to be in control of the people around them. This sounds remarkably similar to the need for alcoholics to wield power over others. Schaafsma says that this is an "important" reason why seats are mounted higher in SUVs than in minivans.

Recall the addict's need to inflate his ego. Controlling others is one way by which to do this. So is having the newest, best, most expensive, powerful and beautiful vehicle, home or toy. While there are plenty of non-addicts holding these as values, we're dealing with probabilities and the weighing of preferences. Understanding, to some degree, the brain of the addict, we can predict that the likelihood of these choices out-weighing practical considerations such as better fuel economy, maneuverability and overall cost of vehicle is greater for the addict than non-addict. Significantly, research reported by Thomas Elliott, Honda's executive Vice-President for North American auto operations, has found that SUV buyers are far more concerned with the vehicle's external appearance, while minivan buyers are more interested in the vehicle's interior and practicality.

Keeping in mind that it is impossible to obtain solid statistics regarding a disease that "nobody has," there is evidence that SUV owners display more signs of addiction in actual driving behaviors than owners of other types of vehicles. A survey by Auto Pacific, Inc., an auto market research company in Santa Monica, CA, found that SUV owners place a lower value on road courtesy than do minivan owners. David Bostwick, DaimlerChrysler's director of market research, found that safety in traffic accidents is not the most important issue for SUV owners as a group. It is the ability to drive in an aggressive manner that concerns them more. Which means, the 5,000 to 7,000 pounds of metal, plastic and rubber are not as important to protect one's self as is the potential to use this against others. Dr. Clotaire Rapaille, a medical anthropologist and consultant to the Big Three U.S. auto makers, points out that SUVs are designed to be masculine, aggressive and assertive, while a minivan evokes images of being married and responsible. Note that aggressive behaviors may include items 1 and 4 through 14 in category one, "Invincibility," along with items 1 through 7 in category two, "Supreme Being complex."

Other evidence includes a finding that multi-tasking is far more common among SUV owners than others.[5] It should also be mentioned that TVs, DVD players, VCRs, positioning computers, etc. are becoming more common in SUVs than in any other vehicle. In addition, SUV owners tend to be less social people, found by the auto makers' marketing studies to be "self-oriented" while minivan buyers tend to be "other-oriented," more involved with community, friends and family.[6] An Auto Club spokesman, commenting on the higher center of gravity resulting in SUVs being twice as likely to be involved in single vehicle accidents (including rollovers and running off the road) suggests that SUV owners learn how to drive these types of vehicles before buying them. He added, "I don't know if (SUV drivers) are aggressive or overconfident in the vehicle's ability but it translates to more dangerous behavior on the road."[7] Aggressiveness and overconfidence are both indications of substance use while driving and therefore, addiction.

Bear in mind that early stage addiction is often marked by ego-fueled over-achievement. As a result, work is the last area of an addict's life to fall apart. The fact that 85% of alcoholics hold jobs supports this idea. Because work provides the funds with which to buy tools and toys including SUVs, these end up further fueling their egos.

1. Support for this is found in Thorburn, *Drunks, Drugs & Debits,* Ibid.

2. Toby Rice Drews, *The 350 Secondary Diseases/Disorders to Alcoholism,* South Plainfield, NJ: Bridge Publishing, 1985.

3. The Wall Street Journal, "The Pride and Joy of a Texan is a Very Big Truck," by Fara Warner, March 29, 1999.

4. New York Times, "Psychological Gulf Separates Minivan, SUV Owners," by Keith Bradsher, late July 2000. This article reports the research that follows, including cites by Schaafsma, Bostwick, Elliott and Rapaille.

5. The Daily News, "Phones, food risky on roads," by Joseph Giordono, November 30, 2000.

6. New York Times, Bradsher, Ibid.

7. The Daily News, "Auto Club suggests tips for SUV owners," by Gregory J. Wilcox, March 6, 1999.

7

Public Policy Suggestions

We now know how to identify likely DUIs. We can see that they are usually addicts in dire need of a reason to change, setting the stage for intervention and sobriety. Only this can help prevent tragedies that are otherwise all but inevitable. It's essential, therefore, to create a system in which addicts are apprehended, dealt appropriate consequences and treated.

Every DUI booked has the potential to save numerous individuals from becoming victim to criminal and/or unethical acts in which the addict almost invariably engages. The DUI is, after all, only the tip of the iceberg and, relative to the number of times it occurs, rarely ends in tragedy. We don't see 90% of what's really going on in the addict's life, whether in the workplace or at home. At the very least, the alcoholic consistently makes life much more difficult for those around him. The on-road attitude is replicated off-road in a much more "up close and personal" way. Loved ones, friends, customers, coworkers, employers, employees, landlords, creditors, defendants to lawsuits and others with whom he comes into contact all suffer. They experience the addict's volatile mood swings, belittling remarks, deceit, outright lies, lack of consideration and dependability, along with a host of other misbehaviors. Even if not a "criminal," he probably regularly drives legally intoxicated. Arresting DUIs is the first line of defense and the most effective offense in the treatment of addiction. Apprehending these drivers in greater numbers may save far more lives and relationships than any other single act in which law enforcers engage.

Yet, according to the DWI Manual, "Some officers are not motivated to detect and arrest DUI violators."[1] I know of several cases in which officers apprehended a DUI, then drove him home instead of keeping him in jail. This is just another way by which addicts are protected from consequences. All enabling needs to stop. Education of law enforcers on alcohol and other drug addiction in the style set forth here may help to create the motivation needed.

Next, the 911 emergency system needs to be improved on a number of levels. Laws need to be changed to allow citizens to follow a DUI suspect while keeping the police dispatcher on-line until an officer is within view. It's amazing, but true, that in some areas the DUI can successfully sue the law enforcement agency and/or the person engaging in pursuit if they become involved in an accident during this process. The courts should not be permitted to entertain such suits unless the pursuit was flagrantly abusive or if the pursuer himself was under the influence.

911 operators need to take any potential DUI very seriously. While many do, I have too often been made to feel as if I am the suspect and queried extensively about why I think the real suspect might be under the influence. The fact that the call is being made should be enough to make law enforcers take notice.

The questions asked of the caller should be kept to a minimum due to the difficulty of driving, calling and gathering information at the same time. For example, rather than asking for additional vehicle identification, it might be more helpful if the operator, after first recording a license plate of a possible DUI, comes back with the question, "Is that a...." giving the make, model and year of the car as confirmation. I found that they can access this information through the license plate alone. Responding in this way would save valuable time, thereby increasing the odds that the culprit is nabbed.

With so many drunk drivers, there are not enough 911 operators and police available to respond to all DUI calls. A system responsible solely for reporting and apprehending possible DUI drivers could be created. As a matter of fact, there are a few police agencies that send reports of vehicle complaints to registered owners when two or more are received. This system could be implemented nationwide with the help of cross-agency referrals. A visit by police to the home of the vehicle's owner could occur after several such complaints by other drivers have been made. This should be done in a non-accusatorial and care-frontational (as opposed to confrontational) way, in which it is pointed out that if the complaints are true, there may be a serious problem with whomever was driving the vehicle at the time. Handbooks could be given to the person or family, along with the suggestion that, if reported again, it will be treated as if DUI is suspected.

Computerization can make it possible to track repeat violators or even one who has been reported in just the last few hours. If emergency operators had immediate access to a database recording this information, it would be easier to prioritize and greatly increase the odds of arresting the most dangerous DUIs.

Those who have a history of vehicle code violations, including even one DUI, could be required to have a prominent sticker on vehicles registered to them with the following notice: "How Am I Driving? Call 800-555-5555 to Report Reckless or Inconsiderate Driving Behaviors." The number given could be that of a special department within the motor vehicle bureau, which would be responsible for determining the authenticity and legitimacy of registered complaints. A letter might be sent to the registered owner for every bonafide complaint, with two or three such calls resulting in a required visit to the local police department and attendance at a driver's education program by the vehicle's owner. If the car is being loaned to a "friend," the first letter may stop this.

Recall the Florida study in which police officers unknowingly released 78% of DUIs after ticketing them for traffic violations. To prevent these mistakes, law enforcers could undergo training to detect likely DUIs based on the driving behaviors discussed in this book and the DWI Manual. They could also learn the behavioral signs of being under the influence. (These symptoms are discussed in great detail in *Drunks, Drugs & Debits*). Finally, they could be trained both to administer the full Standardized Field Sobriety Test, and also to become Drug Recognition Experts.

The eye tracking test, officially known as "horizontal gaze nystagmus," takes only a minute and should be mandatory for all traffic violators and participants in accidents. Due to the workings of the autonomic nervous system, this test is close to foolproof. With alcohol in the system, the eyes begin to shake in a jerking motion when looking to the side, head held straight. Anyone can be trained to measure the angle of deviation from the nose where the shaking begins to occur. This angle determines the BAL, which can be estimated by a properly trained person to a level within .02 per cent of the actual alcohol content proven later by blood testing.

Examining the eyes in this way should be mandatory because, as we said earlier, addicts (like Henri Paul) may not look intoxicated even at very high BALs. Recovering addicts report the countless times they were pulled over, high as a kite and released with only a ticket, not even suspected of DUI. How many addicts have been involved in accidents in which they not only weren't cited but actually sued the other party for causing the accident...and won!? The findings of the Florida study also provide support for administering this simple test. The officers' failures to identify DUIs may not have been a result of bad or incompetent work; it's just that addicts can be superb at appearing sober even when extremely intoxicated. In addition to police attendance at classes describing and explaining the behavioral differences between the early and latter-stage addict, an officer should be required to administer a field sobriety test if requested. Unfortunately, the way things are now, this request can be refused. Even if a citizen asks this of a supervisor, his request may still be denied. Perhaps something could be done about this, also. However, the eye tracking test does not always detect drugs other than alcohol in the system. To remedy this, police officers should have an enforceable right to demand blood, urine or other appropriate samples and test for the presence of such drugs in the system of any traffic violator or participant in a traffic accident. All individuals involved in traffic incidents should have this same right.

Another serious concern is what I like to think of as a misallocation of manpower. Although I am all for police handing out tickets for speeding and other traffic violations, I think that there is a crying need for a certain number of unmarked police vehicles patrolling our roads. These particular law enforcers would have one goal: to apprehend those violators who exhibit the signs of possible DUI discussed in this book.

The reason for the police car being unmarked is that the early-stage addict has trained himself to take notice of the standard markings of law enforcement vehicles. Often, once he sees a cop, he immediately shapes up. If police can spot the addict first, they would have a far better chance of catching him in his true form. Currently, it is estimated that 80% of persons attending traffic school are speed violators. Considering the fact that speeding is only one of many possible indications of DUI (and often not a good one), police may be missing many of the most dangerous violators.

There is also, I feel, a serious failing in the law. In some areas, a conviction for DUI requires proof that the person's ability to safely operate the vehicle is impaired. This standard doesn't account for the early-stage addict who, having extraordinary tolerance, can function exceedingly well at a BAL as high as .24 per cent. Now that we understand addiction, we know that while the addict may display none of the classic signs of inebriation, including staggered gait and slurred speech, he will often engage in reckless behaviors. The standard for conviction of a DUI should be inviolate at .08 per cent or other BAL that takes the behavioral impairments of the addict into account.

Currently, a driver may test at .12 per cent BAL and not be convicted on evidence that he drove, behaved and spoke normally. Yet, the very fact of being pulled over for an infraction is evidence of recklessness, a behavioral impairment with its roots in "ego inflating behaviors."

Even in locations where a .08 BAL convicts with certainty, many officers won't attempt to arrest for DUI because of the extraordinary time it takes to process them. A large percentage of law enforcers feel their time is better spent ticketing more violators. This may be another area where the police need to re-prioritize. Officers should be required to book a suspect once the BAL exceeds a given level.

Furthermore, there is great difficulty in successfully prosecuting a DUI who is not constantly watched between the occurrence of an accident and the arrival of police. A driver later testing at a high BAL may claim he "drank after" the incident. This requires those wishing to have absolute proof of DUI at the time of the accident constantly monitor the suspect. Unfortunately, this can't always be done and most wouldn't think to do so. This could be rectified by a simple change in the law: any alcohol or other drugs found in the system of a person involved in an accident should be assumed to have been there at the time of the incident. A standard accepted allowance for the human liver's ability to process alcohol at about .015 per cent per hour is allowed, but what good is that if the suspect claims he drank after a hit and run, but before being apprehended? If he measures .07 per cent, he should be assumed to have had a BAL of .115 per cent three hours earlier. Until the law is changed we need to watch the person and request that a sobriety test be administered, whenever possible.

One question that needs to be addressed is, how serious an offense should driving under the influence be? There is an argument to be made that being under the influence of any psychoactive drug (including alcohol) while driving should be treated as felony assault. Assault is simply a threat of harm against others. Anyone driving while intoxicated is wielding a dangerous weapon, no different in principal from pointing a loaded gun at someone. Arguably, DUIs could be treated similarly. Of course, there needs to be a reasonable point at which criminal intent is presumed; society has every right to decide the level of risk it will accept and already does so by allowing cars to be driven. Private owners limit this risk to varying degrees; amusement parks set far lower effective blood alcohol limits for customers than do bars and taverns. (Just try acting out in public at a Disneyland theme park in the same way patrons often act inside bars.) There should be some level of alcohol or other drugs in the bloodstream of drivers where the risk is just too great to accept. Whether this is at a .04 or .08 per cent BAL is not within the scope of this book to determine. However, we should consider making this determination when it comes to driving on residential surface streets versus rural two-lane highways, where one slip of the wheel can mean an impact at extremely high speeds and almost certain death. A reasonable rule might allow a BAL no greater than .02 per cent on such highways. Whatever the decision, we should stop making exceptions for the "highly functional" alcoholic as we now do, even if not intended.

The law now generally charges a DUI with a misdemeanor, unless a person has several convictions within a certain number of years or there is an injury due to a DUI-related accident. Why wait for either? Should we prolong the psychological and financial agony of those involved in the addict's life and endanger the lives of those who are unlucky enough to come into physical contact with him? As stated, the earlier consequences can be dealt, the greater the likelihood of permanent sobriety. We need to accept the fact that any person driving in today's anti-drinking and driving culture with a BAL over a certain level (perhaps in the range of .12 to .15 per cent), is probably an alcoholic. As we have shown, pain is the keystone to recovery. Arresting the DUI is the best way to administer that pain. Friends and family need to be educated in the idea that they should not enable the addict by posting bail or "helping" him in any way. We need to understand that friends do let friends plead guilty and that they may even want to consider reporting a friend to help prevent a future tragedy.

While the convicted should be encouraged to attend A.A. or other programs of sobriety, he cannot be forced to accept the ideas presented. These programs only work when the addict has experienced enough pain in his life to be willing to make the change. Sobriety, however, should be required for any special treatment under the law. Since active addiction likely caused the behaviors, there needs to be some form of enforced abstinence. Regular and random blood/urine testing should be required as a condition for early release or any period of probation. If there is any failure of these tests while incarcerated, the prisoner should not be released early. For a failure to remain sober during a period of probation, he should be sent back to prison to serve out his original term. This gives the addict a choice and even an incentive to stay the path of abstinence and, hopefully, recovery.

The reason choices need to be offered has to do with the psychology of the typical inmate and regular rule violator. Most of these are of a Temperament who, if they are "punished" in the classic sense, will strike back. Punishment needs to be carefully thought out and used sparingly. The connection needs to be made between a violation in which there was harm (or threat thereof) against others and a logical, appropriate consequence. A persuasive argument can be made that most prisoners are addicts. Most began addictive use of drugs in early adolescence (usually during the first drinking episode) at the average age of 13 in the United States. Recovering addicts tell us that their own emotional growth stopped at that point. Therefore, the emotional age of the typical addict, as well as most prisoners, is that of a child. "Logical consequences" are the best method by which to deal with the resulting unruly behavior.[2]

There is also a concern with the criminal justice system in general. Since addiction usually begins in the early teen years, adolescents more often decide on their occupational or professional choices at a point long after addiction is triggered. The question for addicts becomes, consciously or not, "How can I best inflate my ego?" In what occupation or profession can the addict wield power over others? It is not a coincidence that five out of eight 20th Century Nobel Prize winning authors from the United States were alcoholics. What better way for those with the gift of communication to wield power over minds? It also shouldn't come as a surprise that 30% of Academy Award winning actors have been identified as alcohol and other drug addicts.[3] These celebrities control their audiences and fans. Neither is it shocking that 80-90% of those who impose coercion over others criminally, are addicts.

Unfortunately, some addicts choose law enforcement as their way of wielding power. As we have seen, destructive behaviors often don't just occur during drinking episodes and do not even happen every time an alcoholic drinks to an inebriated state. However, some Drug Recognition Expert police officers report that, depending on the size and location of the department, 20-50% of their fellow officers are believed to have been or still are active alcoholics. Even law enforcers, when addicts, will, at least occasionally, act destructively. It is when these officers engage in such behaviors that jurors and other citizens begin to distrust all police. There is also anecdotal evidence that at some prisons as many as half of the guards may be practicing alcoholics. This could explain many of the serious problems that occur at some jails.

This idea can be extended to addicts in government, where power can become a life and death matter for civilians. Any ranking official (including police) suspected of improprieties in either his personal or professional life could also be identified as having the disease of alcoholism, since that is usually the source of serious problems. Those suspected should be dealt with appropriately and swiftly, with required alcohol and other drug testing. Alcohol diversion classes and rehabilitation with 12-Step Program attendance should also be recommended.

There may even be cause to implement random and regular blood/urine testing of all persons in every branch of law enforcement. This would include police, prison guards, judges and administrative personnel. There is a far higher probability that practicing addicts in such positions of power will engage in corrupt activities than recovering or non-addicts. Practicing alcoholics who arrest alcoholics, who in turn are guarded by alcoholics, is not a system that promotes rehabilitation. Nor is it one that would be expected to properly mete out justice. Any law enforcer arriving to work at a .08 per cent BAL or greater should be treated as an alcoholic. Anything over .03 per cent should be at least suspect. If alcohol is found during working hours and the behavioral signs of addiction are evident,[4] a cause and effect relationship between use and behaviors should be assumed unless proven otherwise.

We've all heard about the "war on drugs." If it is a war, it seems to be one we can't win. Some of the reasons for this include a 10,000-mile border that can't be adequately policed, combined with an amazing ability of drug merchants to regularly create new synthetic products. Question: is it possible that we are focusing on the wrong thing? Maybe the criminal justice system needs to punish the behaviors and not the use and concentrate on demand rather than supply. We might want to consider narrowing the scope of the war on drugs by looking at the people who, due to a biological predisposition, process drugs—including alcohol—in a way that causes them to engage in destructive behaviors. In other words, the addicts. Those who endanger or harm others need to be caught, prosecuted and given appropriate consequences. This change of focus may free up resources necessary to provide more training to police officers, as well as better treatment facilities.

We may never keep the addict from drinking and/or using by threat of law. The fact that doctors supply far more addicts with legal psychoactive drugs than street dealers sell of their less socially acceptable brands is proof of this. School kids age 12 and even younger can obtain illicit drugs within minutes of arriving in a city they've never before visited. I'll say it again: if we narrow the focus of the "war on drugs" to those who act destructively and in ways that cause others to suffer, an opportunity will be provided to turn what may be perceived as failure into success.

Figure 4

	Summary of Public Policy Proposals
1	Send other drivers' complaints of reckless driving to the registered vehicle owner.
2	Institute a system in which multiple complaints of inconsiderate/reckless driving behaviors results in care-frontational meetings with the registered vehicle owner by law enforcers.
3	Track complaints by vehicle license. Put those for whom there have been repeated complaints on "high priority" status for apprehension.
4	Require a "How Am I Driving?" sticker on all vehicles involved in previous DUI convictions or frequent other vehicle code violations.

Summary of Public Policy Proposals (continued)

5	Mandate that all police officers be required to attend classes describing and explaining the disparate behaviors of early and latter stage addicts.
6	Make testing for eye nystagmus mandatory for all traffic violators and participants to accidents.
7	Allow police officers an enforceable right to demand body fluid tests for any traffic violators/participants in accidents.
8	Allow any party to a traffic accident an enforceable right to demand such testing.
9	Allow unmarked police cars to apprehend possible DUIs.
10	To increase the odds of arresting DUIs, put more emphasis on apprehending non-speeding law violators.
11	Motivate officers to apprehend and arrest DUI suspects.
12	Allow citizens to follow DUI suspects when speaking with a 911 operator until the suspect is apprehended by police.
13	Strictly limit possible lawsuits against private persons engaging in safe pursuit of a possible DUI.
14	Create an alternative system to 911 solely for apprehending DUIs.
15	Require officers to book legally intoxicated suspects.
16	Any alcohol or other drugs found in the system of a person involved in an accident should be assumed to have been there at the time of the incident.
17	DUIs with a BAL over a certain level should be treated as felony assault.
18	Create "ZERO-BAL" zones on particularly dangerous highways.
19	Connect the dots for the convicted criminal between use of a substance and his having come into contact with the criminal justice system.
20	Require regular and random alcohol and other drug testing for convicted criminals wishing to avoid or decrease time spent in jail, and as a condition of an extended period of parole.
21	Those on parole found drinking or using should be sent back to prison to serve out their original term.
22	Narrow the scope of the war on drugs to those who act destructively toward others.

1. *DWI Manual,* Ibid., p. II-4.
2. *The Role of Type and Temperament in Diagnosing and Treating Addiction,* Ibid.; support found in Delunas, Dreikurs, Thorburn and Keirsey.
3. Lucy Barry Robe, *Co-Starring Famous Women and Alcohol: The Dramatic Truth Behind the Tragedies and Triumphs of 200 Celebrities,* Minneapolis, MI: CompCare Publications, 1986.
4. Described in detail by Doug Thorburn in *Drunks, Drugs & Debits,* Ibid.

Epilogue

In May, 1998 Illinois State Trooper Lonnie Murbarger arrested Tasha French for driving under the influence. At the time of her apprehension French told Murbarger that he was "ruining her life." With nine years on the force, Murbarger had busted a lot of intoxicated drivers and had heard many similar tirades. He never heard back from any of those whom he had jailed for DUI.

July 11, 2001 proved to be an exception. French, in her 20s, not only thanked Murbarger for her arrest, but also presented him with a plaque. Initially he was skeptical and even reluctant to accept the award. His reticence melted when French explained, "If you hadn't arrested me...I'd be dead from drinking by now."

Tasha's family, friends and others unknown--all potential victims of the biological way in which she processes alcohol--were also beneficiaries to Murbarger's intervention.

Murbarger and other officers like him deserve not only the support, but also the gratitude of everyone who comes in contact with the addict. Recovering alcoholics can lead the way in supporting the officers who put their lives on the line when dealing with addicts in pre-recovery. This may involve expanding the concept of the Ninth Step in the 12-Step program of Alcoholics Anonymous.

Step Nine calls for paying amends to those harmed by the misbehaviors of the addict while still drinking and using. It requires contrition on the part of the addict, something that is truly beautiful to experience when properly carried out. An appropriate adjunct to a deep, sincere apology would be a heartfelt "thank you" to those who helped to administer the pain needed to create the motivation to become abstinent and, eventually, sober. Tasha French set the standard for every recovering addict to achieve.

The 12-Step Program works as well as it does because it helps to both deflate the massive alcoholic ego and rebuild the addict's zeroed-out self-esteem. Thanking those who meted out consequences would add immeasurably to advancing these twin goals. Also, non-addicts need the emotional and intellectual support for having done what, for them, may have seemed like a superhuman feat. After all, sober humans generally don't want to hurt others. We need to understand that experiencing consequences is the one thing addicts need most. Such "thanks" would not only advance the education of non-addicts about the proper treatment of addiction, but would also act as reinforcement for offering this type of uncompromising tough love in the future, when the opportunity is again presented.

Cell Phone Note

As mentioned throughout this book, a wireless phone can be an important tool in the apprehension of intoxicated drivers. On numerous occasions my wireless phone has played an important role in averting possible tragedies on the road. I strongly recommend the purchase of such a device to anyone interested in protecting themselves and others from the dangerous behaviors of DUIs.

Those who don't wish to purchase a cell phone requiring a minimum monthly subscription may wish to consider shelling out a one-time fee for a phone that is capable of only calling 911. Such a device is available. Magnavox® Mobile 911™ is one such wireless phone without monthly service fees. In addition to being able to call 911 from anywhere in the United States where analog cellular phones operate, it is equipped with a 95-decibel siren, useful either in attracting attention to an emergency or scaring someone away. At $199, you'll spend less than you would on a standard cellular phone in just seven to ten months. The toll free number through which to obtain this emergency phone is (800) 922-2966, or visit www.comtrad.com.

Appendix One -- Clues to DUI

A Sense of Invincibility--Chapter 2

1. Speeding recklessly through traffic.
2. Not wearing a seat belt.
3. Doing several things at once ("multi-tasking"), such as driving, putting on make-up, reading the paper, eating, smoking, changing radio stations and using a mobile phone.
4. On a mobile phone and either attempting to do anything else and/or engaging in any degree of reckless driving behavior.
5. Speeding up to make the light after it's turned red.
6. Markedly speeding up, crossing a yellow light and barely making it.
7. Speeding up to make a left turn in front of someone with inadequate distance.
8. Turning with excessive speed (35% probability of DUI according to the NHTSA study).
9. Tailgating (50% probability), while not trying too hard to get around traffic.
10. Excessive speed with a child in the vehicle.
11. Speeding at 25 mph or more over the speed limit.
12. Passing on a two-lane highway over a solid yellow line.
13. Passing quickly to the left before the official left-hand turn lane.
14. Excessive speed in inclement weather, including fog, snow or ice.

Supreme Being Complex Clues--Chapter 3

1. Tailgating, (50% probability) while speeding and obviously trying to get through traffic.
2. Obscene gestures (60% probability).
3. Road rage.
4. Cutting a tight corner combined with speeding during a left

turn.

5. Not yielding the right-of-way, (45% probability) especially with an attitude.

6. Cutting in line.

7. Passing to the right in a right-hand turn lane, without turning right.

8. Littering.

9. Windows tinted to the point where we can't see the driver's face.

10. Driving alone in a lane requiring at least two people.

11. Parking in a handicapped space without a placard or disability.

12. Unnecessarily taking up two parking spaces.

13. Evading tolls at a tollbooth.

Poor Judgment, Leading to Increased Risk of Driver Error--Chapter 4

1. Almost striking an object, vehicle or person (60% probability).

2. Actually striking an object, vehicle or person.

3. Inability to multi-task.

4. One set of tires on a line (45% probability).

5. Straddling line, with the center or lane marker in-between the wheels (65% probability).

6. Driving on a shoulder (55% probability).

7. Abruptly swerving (55% probability).

8. Drifting(50% probability).

9. Riding the brakes (45% probability).

10. Unnecessary braking (45% probability).

11. Backing into traffic (45% probability).

12. Slow response to traffic signal (40% probability).

13. Accelerating or decelerating much more rapidly than traffic conditions require (30% probability).

14. Positioning to accelerate and decelerate rapidly (30% probability).

15. Stopping abruptly (30% probability), not at an intersection (as in stop and go traffic).

16. Stopping too abruptly (30% probability) at an intersection.

17. Poor merging.

18. Turning with a wide radius ("squaring the turn") (65% proba-

bility).
19. Running a red light, but not speeding up to do so.
20. Making a left turn in front of someone with inadequate distance.
21. Failing to yield the right of way, but without an attitude.
22. Unusually slow in pulling over for an emergency vehicle.
23. Passing on a two-lane highway with inadequate distance.
24. Weaving (60% probability).

Apparent Mental Confusion--Chapter 5

1. Erratic gestures.
2. Driving in the turn-only lane, straight, without turning (55% probability).
3. Driving slower than 10 mph below the speed limit (50% probability).
4. Stopping without cause in a traffic lane (50% probability).
5. Erratic braking (45% probability).
6. Driving the wrong way on a one-way street (45% probability).
7. Signaling inconsistent with one's actions (40% probability).
8. Stopping far short of an intersection (35% probability).
9. Stopping inappropriately at a crosswalk (35% probability).
10. Stopping for a green light, or for a flashing yellow (35% probability).
11. Illegal or abrupt turn (35% probability).
12. Turning sharply from a wrong lane (35% probability).
13. Illegal U-turn (35% probability).
14. Turning from outside a designated turn lane (35% probability).
15. Headlights not on when required (30% probability).
16. Erratic movements inside the vehicle.

Physical Signs of Person or Vehicle--Chapter 6

1. Smoking.
2. Chewing gum combined with any reckless behavior, poor judgment or evidence of mental confusion.
3. Window wide open on a hot or cold day combined with any reckless behavior, poor judgement or evidence of mental confusion.

4. Drinking anything combined with any reckless behavior, poor judgment or evidence of mental confusion.

5. Head out the window (60% probability).

6. Tightly gripping the wheel (60% probability).

7. Slouching in the seat (60% probability).

8. Face close to windshield (60% probability).

9. Eye fixation (60% probability).

10. Covering one eye with the hand or closing one eye.

11. Any other physical clue that suggests the driver appears to be drunk (60% probability).

12. Extremely loud music combined with any reckless behavior, poor judgment or evidence of mental confusion.

13. Flashy or very large vehicle combined with any reckless behavior, poor judgment or evidence of mental confusion.

14. Looks like a "druggie" type.

15. Vehicle with lots of nicks and dents combined with any reckless behavior, poor judgment or evidence of mental confusion.

16. Vehicle obviously not taken care of combined with any reckless behavior, poor judgment or evidence of mental confusion.

17. SUV combined with any reckless behavior, poor judgment or evidence of mental confusion.

Bibliography

Alcoholics Anonymous: The Story of How Many Thousands of Men and Women Have Recovered from Alcoholism, New York: Alcoholics Anonymous World Services, Inc., Third Edition, 1990.

Amundson, Everett R., *Responsible Driving,* Whittier, CA: Everett R. Amundson, 1995.

Behr, Edward, *Prohibition: Thirteen Years That Changed America,* New York: Arcade Publishing, 1996.

Black, Claudia, *Children of Alcoholics -- As Youngsters -- Adolescents -- Adults -- It Will Never Happen to Me!,* New York: Ballantine Books, 1981.

Braun, Stephen, *Buzz: The Science and Lore of Alcohol and Caffeine,* New York, Oxford University Press, 1996.

Cassingham, Randy, internet site *www.thisistrue.com*

Delunas, Eve, *Survival Games Personalities Play,* Carmel, CA: SunInk Publications, 1992.

Dreikurs, Rudolf, MD, *Children: The Challenge,* New York: The Penguin Group, 1990.

Drews, Toby Rice, *The 350 Secondary Diseases/Disorders to Alcoholism,* South Plainfield, NJ: Bridge Publishing, 1980.

Fairhurst, Alice and Lisa L. Fairhurst, *Effective Teaching, Effective Learning,* Palo Alto, CA: Davies-Black Publishing (Consulting Psychologist Press, Inc.), 1995.

Fitzgerald, Kathleen Whalen, Ph.D., *Alcoholism: the Genetic Inheritance,* New York: Doubleday, 1988.

Goodwin, Donald, M.D., *Is Alcoholism Hereditary?*, New York: Ballantine Books, 1988.

Gorski, Terence and Merlene Miller, *Staying Sober: A Guide for Relapse Prevention,* Independence, MO: Herald House/ Independence Press, 1986.

Gorski, Terence, *Do Family of Origin Problems Cause Chemical Addiction?*, Independence, MO: Herald House/Independence Press, 1989.

Graham, James, *The Secret History of Alcoholism: The Story of Famous Alcoholics and Their Destructive Behavior*, Rockport, MA: Element Books, 1996. Also published as, *Vessels of Rage, Engines of Power: The Secret History of Alcoholism*, Lexington, VA: Aculeus Press, 1994.

Johnson, Vernon E., *I'll Quit Tomorrow*, San Francisco, CA: Harper and Row, 1980.

Knapp, Caroline, *Drinking: A Love Story*, New York: The Dial Press, 1996.

LAPD Website, www.cityofla.org/LAPD/traffic/dre/drgdrvr.htm: Thomas E. Page, "The Drug Recognition Expert's (DREs) Response to the Drug Impaired Driver."

Martin, Father Joseph C., *Chalk Talks on Alcohol*, San Francisco, CA: Harper and Row, 1989.

Milam, Dr. James R. and Katherine Ketcham, *Under the Influence: A Guide to the Myths and Realities of Alcoholism,* New York: Bantam Books, 1983.

Morrison, Martha, *White Rabbit: A Doctor's Story of Her Addiction and Recovery*, New York: Crown Publishers, 1989.

Robe, Lucy Barry, *Co-starring Famous Women and Alcohol: the*

Dramatic Truth Behind the Tragedies and Triumphs of 200 Celebrities, Minneapolis, MN: CompCare Publications, 1986.

Roy, Maria, Ed., *Battered Women: A Psychosociological Study of Domestic Violence,* New York: Van Nostrand, 1977.

Royce, James E. and David Scratchly, *Alcoholism and Other Drug Problems,* New York: The Free Press, 1996.

Tennant, Forest, M.D., Dr. P.H., *Medical Uses and Legal Identification of Drug Use,* videotape series, West Covina, CA: Veract, Inc.

U.S. Department of Transportation, *DWI Detection and Standardized Field Sobriety Testing: Student Manual,* Oklahoma City, OK: National Highway Traffic Safety Administration, 1995.

Wooden, Kenneth, *the Children of Jonestown,* New York: McGraw-Hill, 1981.

Index

Praise for
Drunks, Drugs & Debits:
How to Recognize Addicts
and Avoid Financial Abuse
by Doug Thorburn

"...your book probably saved my sanity, and possibly will save my life..."

Mary F.

"A signal public service."

Nick Avery

"The most valuable book I've ever read except the Bible."

Anonymous, M.D.

"The book is so unusual and so valuable I bought two. It should be required reading in schools and every businessman should study it. "

Jeff Barnes

"*Drunks, Drugs & Debits* gave me tremendous insight into behaviors of family and acquaintances that previously were beyond my comprehension. It freed me from the enabling cycle."

Joyce Kaszynski

"This was a great book with a unique perspective. It gave me a whole new way to look at the situation. Doug Thorburn obviously knows his subject very well."

Yvonne Pover

"The book's list of identifying attributes came my way in time for me not to marry into a lifetime of abuse. I had no idea that the man I loved was two different people until I read this book."

49 year old professional

"*Drunks, Drugs & Debits* is a wonderfully insightful read into what can otherwise be incomprehensible behaviors."

Jeannette Drouin Graham

"This book is not only the foundation of understanding addiction and its affects on society, but it is also the first step in educating people at all levels, a key component in eradicating a problem."

Yvan Auger

"Great book!"

Paul Dewey Holzer, CDS, CATS Counselor

"This book was a terrific eye-opener."

Ken Schoolland, Professor and Author

"Doug Thorburn offers a unique perspective on alcoholism specifically and drug addiction in general. I highly recommend this unique, eye-opening book."
Katherine Ketcham, co-author of *Under the Influence*

"*Must* reading for anyone fearing that they are detrimentally involved with an addicted person."
Midwest Book Review

"...should lead to a revolution in several applied sciences, including psychiatry, psychology, criminology and medicine."
Robert Prechter, *The Elliott Wave Theorist*

"If you've ever wanted to know WHY someone near you did some inexplicably stupid or mean thing to you, you've GOT to read this book. You will find that 'you know a LOT more addicts than you think.'"
Randy Cassingham, internet columnist
THISisTRUE.com and *HeroicStories.com*

"A vital resource for psychotherapists."
Eve Delunas, PH.D., Marriage and Family Therapist (CA), author, *Survival Games Personalities Play*

"One of the most important books ever written. A must read for all who want to understand the ways and wayward inclinations of the alcohol and other drug addict."
Dr. Forest Tennant, M.D., Dr. P.H.,
President, Veract, Inc.

"An important book for all financial planning practitioners to read."
Colin B. Coombs, CLU, CFP

"Truly excellent. Doug has my professional admiration."
James Crossen, professor of Addiction Studies,
Pierce College, Woodland Hills

"Told with passion and backed with facts, *Drunks, Drugs & Debits* is a compelling look into the relationships among addiction, finances and personality."
Alice M. and Lisa L. Fairhurst, authors, *Effective Teaching, Effective Learning: Making the Personality Connection in Your Classroom*

"An entirely fresh look...Outstanding!"
Audrey DeLaMarte, reviewer for
The Phoenix and *Steps to Recovery*

"I very much enjoyed reading about the far reaching effects of addiction as discussed in this book. ...could easily be a curriculum for alcoholics, addicts, counselors, codependents, lawyers, accountants and many others."
Cardwell C. Nuckols, Ph. D.

"This book will allow managers to identify addiction early and possibly even screen out employees in the hiring process."
Tom Reilly, Manager

Order Form

Fax Orders: 818.363.3111
Phone Orders: 818.360.0985
Website: www.PrevenTragedy.com
E-mail Orders: PrevenTragedy@mindspring.com
Postal Orders: Galt Publishing; P.O. Box 7777; Northridge, CA 91327

Please send _____ copies of "Drunks, Drugs & Debits" @ $29.95 each

$_____

Please send _____ copies of "Get Out of the Way!" @ $12.95 each

$_____

Sales Tax: please add 8.25% for books shipped to California addresses

$_____

"We pay shipping"

Total Investment $_____

I wish to pay by:
        _____ Check Enclosed
        _____ Visa   _____ Mastercard   _____ Discover
                Card Number: _____ _____ _____ _____ Exp. ___/___
                Name on Card: _____
                Signature (required): _____

Deliver to: Name _____
        Address _____
        City _____ State ___ Zip Code _____

Telephone Number : _____
E-mail Address (for updates): _____

Please send additional information on:
                _____ Drunks, Drugs & Debits
                _____ Speaking & Seminars
                _____ Quantity prices on books

Drunks, Drugs & Debits is a 362-page hardcover book that provides a detailed, in-depth view of alcohol and other drug addiction as it applies to all areas of one's life.